CARLTON FREDERICKS'
SODIUM COUNTER

ALSO BY CARLTON FREDERICKS

New Low Blood Sugar and You
Low Blood Sugar and You
Look Younger, Feel Healthier
Carlton Fredericks' Low Carbohydrate Diet
Carlton Fredericks' Cookbook for Good Nutrition
The Low Blood Sugar Cookbook
Psychonutrition
Winning the Fight Against Breast Cancer
Eat Well, Stay Well
Arthritis: You Don't Have to Learn to Live With It
Carlton Fredericks' Guide to Women's Nutrition

CARLTON FREDERICKS'
SODIUM COUNTER

A PERIGEE BOOK

Perigee Books
are published by
The Putnam Publishing Group
200 Madison Avenue
New York, NY 10016

Library of Congress Cataloging-in-Publication Data

Fredericks, Carlton.
[Sodium counter]
Carlton Fredericks' sodium counter.
p. cm.
1. Food—Sodium content—Tables. I. Title.
II. Title: Sodium counter.
TX553.S65F74 1989   88-25574 CIP
641.1′7—dc19

ISBN 0-399-51509-7

Printed in the United States of America
1   2   3   4   5   6   7   8   9   10

INTRODUCTION

Salt, the second leading food additive in the American diet (sugar is the first), is composed largely of sodium, which has increasingly become a concern to nutritionists. Dr. Carlton Fredericks agrees with other members of the medical community that the "evidence suggests that a high-sodium diet may contribute to the development of high blood pressure." High blood pressure increases the risk of strokes and heart and kidney disease, so this concern is not unwarranted.

Diets high in sodium are relatively recent. Salt was a rare and expensive commodity for most of its 6,000 year history. Our ancestors received an adequate supply of sodium (the body requires 300 mgs. daily) from foods in which it occurred naturally, like milk, cheese, vegetables, and meats.

Salt, obtained either by the evaporation of sea water or from hills of salt discovered in desert countries, was first used to preserve meat and fish from spoiling. Its preserving qualities were so revered, in fact, that many groups attributed spiritual powers to it as well. The Egyptians rubbed it on their coffins in the belief that it would help preserve their souls. Covenants were sealed over a sacrificial meal in which salt was a necessary ingredient.

But the taste salt imparted to the food it preserved was also quickly appreciated and it became even more sought after but, nonetheless, still difficult to obtain. Roads had to be built to transport the salt. One of the oldest roads in Italy is the Via Salaria (Salt Route) over which salt was carried to various parts of the country. Roman officers in foreign countries were given an extra allowance to purchase the salt they desired to flavor their foods (this is the origin of the English word "salary"). In the Middle Ages, only royalty enjoyed the luxury of a saltshaker. Until 300 years ago, salt was neither accessible nor affordable to most people.

Today, however, salt—and thus sodium—is almost unavoidable in our society. The average American consumes between 4,000 and 8,000 mgs. of sodium (2 to 4 teaspoons of salt) per day. The National Research Council of the National Academy of Sciences sets the safe sodium-intake level at between 1,100 and 3,300 mgs. of sodium daily. While this is above our actual body requirement, doctors recommend this level to satisfy our body's need for other nutrients.

The main source of our elevated levels of sodium is not the salt we use in cooking or what we sprinkle on our food. The Center for Science in the Public Interest says this accounts for only 15 percent of our daily sodium intake. Nor is it the sodium occurring naturally in some foods, which accounts for another 10 percent. The bulk is from processed foods that make up over half our diet each day.

Salt is used extensively as a taste enhancer and a preservative in processed foods, with an additional 10 percent coming from other sodium-containing additives. These additives include baking powder and baking soda used in the making of bread and other baked goods, brine used in pickling, monosodium glutamate (MSG) used as a taste intensifier, and other preservatives such as sodium nitrite, sodium benzoate, and sodium sulfite.

The implications for our diet become clear when one compares the sodium content of some of the food we eat. A bowl of regular oatmeal contains 2 mgs. of sodium, while instant oatmeal has 379 mgs. One cup of fresh cooked peas has 2 mgs., and canned peas has 400 mgs. Two slices of bread contain approximately 300 mgs. of sodium, three ounces of tuna in oil 530 mgs., and a frankfurter has over 500 mgs., depending on the brand. A McDonald's Big Mac contains 1,010 mgs. Have a Chef Boyardee spaghetti and meatball dinner and you consume 900 mgs.

The problems associated with excessive sodium are connected to the reasons why sodium is essential to good health. Sodium maintains blood volume and blood pressure by attracting and holding water in the blood vessels. It also plays an important role, along with chloride and potassium, in maintaining the balance between acids and bases in our body fluids. This is the electrolyte balance, which is essential in the maintenance of all our body functions.

Nature has provided us with machinery to maintain normal levels of sodium—our kidneys. When the body has too much sodium, the kidneys excrete it through the urine. When the body needs more, the kidneys reabsorb it from the urine and filter it back to the blood. But the demand on our kidneys is far greater than ever before and the kidneys of many people cannot excrete all the sodium.

And this is where the connection between sodium and hypertension begins. Excess sodium in the body causes the amount of water in and around body tissues to increase. The volume of blood in the circulating system also increases. Blood vessels become constricted, making it harder for the increased amount of blood to pass through the vessels. This condition, in turn, elevates blood pressure and heart rate. To reduce the flow of blood, the body establishes a cycle of constricting the blood vessels, which puts the body in a hypertensive state.

Studies of primitive populations confirm this. In the *Nutrition Guide for the Prevention and Cure of Common Ailments and Diseases*, Carlton Fredericks describes two groups of people, one cooking with ocean water, high in salt, the other with fresh water. "The former," he says, "experience our toll of hypertension, while the other group is not only free of it but displays a drop in blood pressure with aging. This is diametrically opposed to what happens," he adds, "in salt-soaked civilization, where for decades we were told that the 'normal' blood pressure is one's age plus 100—a formula that really means that we grow sicker as we grow older."

Other factors also effect the state of hypertension, including the sodium-potassium relationship. If sodium constricts arteries in the body's arterial system, potassium enlarges arteries in that same system. If blood pressure is raised, increasing the potassium level in the body could improve the effect of a low-salt diet, used to lower blood pressure. Unfortunately, as Dr. Fredericks points out, food processing "defeats us on both points. If you look up the sodium and potassium values of a fresh vegetable, and compare them with those of a canned or frozen version of the same food, you frequently find that the potassium content has been lowered in processing and the sodium value raised."

What alternatives are available to us?

- Become an educated consumer. Use the charts in this book when shopping and preparing meals. Read labels. Become aware of the sodium content of the foods you eat and drink most often.
- During times when your body tends to retain sodium—just before the start of the menstrual period—avoid giving in to cravings for salt.
- Try some of the numerous salt-free cookbooks now available. Follow some of the suggestions offered by Dr. Ralph E. Minear in his book, *The Joy of Living Salt-Free.* Eliminate the saltshaker from the table and don't use it in cooking. Use fresh vegetables whenever possible. Frozen vegetables are second choice. Avoid canned ones. Avoid prepared dinners, soups, and sauces unless marked "low sodium." Add flavor with spices such as ginger, bay leaf, pepper. Use oil, vinegar, and lemon.
- Avoid adding salt to food you serve children, recommends

Dr. Fredericks. "Some researchers have suggested that the high-sodium intake of adults is the result of acquiring a taste for sodium through exposure to high-sodium foods during childhood."

And as Dr. Fredericks concisely sums up, "In a nutrition-conscious society, trying to avoid sugar, alcohol, and additives . . . why add sodium when it's not needed?"

Some Notes for The Sodium Counter

The user of this book should be aware (and probably is) that the sodium content in natural foods varies from one harvest to another and that the amounts in this booklet are approximate, even those given for unprocessed foods, such as beef, vegetables, and fresh milk. During the course of researching this book, I became aware that so-called "diet foods," those which are designated "lo cal" or "lite" or other such labels indicating a reduction in calories and/or fat, *frequently*, but not always, contain more salt than the same product not so designated. The person on a low-salt diet who is also trying to reduce calorie intake should check the labels of such products before making a selection. The probable reason for more salt is its flavor enhancing properties.

To be correct, this book should be called *The Sodium Chloride Counter* or *The Salt Counter*. Sodium is a metal which is actually derived from salt. The Columbia Encyclopedia defines salt as "a common and widely used substance, chemically a compound of the elements sodium and chloride called sodium chloride. . . . The compound is important in many ways. It is the chief source of the metal sodium and of its compounds, such as baking soda and caustic soda."

ABBREVIATIONS AND SYMBOLS

& = and
c = cup
fl = fluid
gm = gram, grams
" = inch
med = medium
oz = ounce
pkg = package
pc = piece
pt = pint
lb = pound
qt = quart
tbs = tablespoon
tsp = teaspoon

EQUIVALENTS

By Weight

1 ounce = 28.35 grams
3.52 ounces = 100 grams
1 pound = 16 ounces

By Volume

1 tablespoon = 3 tea-
spoons
2 tablespoons = 1 fluid
ounce
1 cup = 8 fluid ounces
1 cup = ½ pint
1 cup = 16 tablespoons
1 pound butter = 4 sticks
or 2 cups
1 quart = 4 cups

A

	Serving Size	Sodium (mgs)
AC'CENT FLAVOR ENHANCER	½ tsp	300
ANGEL FOOD CAKE MIXES (*General Mills*)	¹⁄₁₂ pkg	300
ARMOUR DINNER CLASSICS. SEE ENTRIES UNDER DINNERS, FROZEN.		

B

	Serving Size	Sodium (mgs)
BACON (*See Breakfast Meats*)		
BAKING POWDER (*Davis*)	1 tsp	330
BARBECUE SAUCE* (*Open Pit*)		
Hickory Smoke Flavor	1 tbs	230
Hot 'n Tangy Flavor	1 tbs	210
Mesquite 'n Tangy Flavor	1 tbs	250
Original Flavor	1 tbs	250
Original Flavor with Minced Onions	1 tbs	270
Sweet 'n Tangy Flavor	1 tbs	190
Thick 'n Tangy Hickory Flavor	1 tbs	230
BEANS, CANNED		
B&M Baked Beans		
Barbecue Baked Beans	8 oz	960
Honey Baked Beans	8 oz	940
Red Kidney Baked Beans	8 oz	640
Small Pea Baked Beans	8 oz	750
Tomato Baked Beans	8 oz	1010
Vegetarian Baked Beans	8 oz	750
Yellow Eye Baked Beans	8 oz	770
Campbell's		
Barbecue Beans	7⅞ oz	900
Home Style Beans	8 oz	900

*See also Hunt's Products.

	Serving Size	Sodium (mgs)
Old Fashioned Beans in Molasses and Brown Sugar	8 oz	730
Pork and Beans in Tomato Sauce	8 oz	740
Ranchero Beans	7⅞ oz	900
Progresso		
Black-Eyed Peas	8 oz	N.A.
Black Turtle Beans	8 oz	N.A.
Cannellini (White Kidney Beans)	8 oz	717
Chick Peas (Ceci)	8 oz	691
Fava Beans	8 oz	N.A.
Red Kidney Beans	8 oz	1080
Roman Beans	8 oz	N.A.
Pinto Beans	8 oz	N.A.
Van Camp's		
Baked Beans	1 c	1010
Beanee Weenee	1 c	990
Brown Sugar Beans	1 c	690
Butter Beans	1 c	750
Dark Red Kidney Beans	1 c	730
Light Red Kidney Beans	1 c	690
Mexican Style Kidney Beans	1 c	720
New Orleans Style Red Kidney Beans	1 c	790
Pork and Beans	1 c	1010
Red Beans	1 c	930
BEEF STEW		
Dinty Moore (24 oz)	8 oz	980
Dinty Moore (40 oz)	8 oz	971
Wolf Brand	scant c	1041
BISCUITS (*Pillsbury*)		
Big Country Buttermilk	2 biscuits	650
Butter	2 biscuits	360
Buttermilk	2 biscuits	360

N.A.: This information is not available.

	Serving Size	Sodium (mgs)
Country	2 biscuits	360
Extra Lights Flaky Buttermilk	2 biscuits	360
Tenderflake Baking Powder Dinner	2 biscuits	340
Hungry Jack		
Buttermilk Flaky	2 biscuits	590
Buttermilk Fluffy	2 biscuits	560
Butter Tastin' Flaky	2 biscuits	310
Deluxe Heat 'n Eat Buttermilk	2 biscuits	610
Extra Rich Buttermilk	2 biscuits	350
Flaky	2 biscuits	590
Heat 'n Eat Buttermilk	2 biscuits	610

BLUE BONNET. (*See entries for Margarine.*)

BOLOGNA. (*See entries for Luncheon Meats.*)

BREAD MIXES

Dromedary		
Corn Bread (prepared)*	2″ × 2″ pc	480
Gingerbread (prepared)*	2″ × 2″ pc	190
Pound Cake (prepared)*	½″ slice	160
Quick Mixes (*Pillsbury*)		
Applesauce Spice	¹/₁₂ loaf	150
Apricot Nut	¹/₁₂ loaf	150
Banana	¹/₁₂ loaf	200
Blueberry Nut	¹/₁₂ loaf	150
Carrot Nut	¹/₁₂ loaf	180
Cherry Nut	¹/₁₂ loaf	140
Cranberry	¹/₁₂ loaf	150
Date	¹/₁₂ loaf	150
Honey Granola	¹/₁₂ loaf	160
Nut	¹/₁₂ loaf	140

*Does not include sodium in water used to prepare. Local water supplies vary in sodium content.

	Serving Size	Sodium (mgs)
BREAKFAST MEATS		
Bacon (*Oscar Mayer*) after cooking	1 slice (6 gm)	120
⅛" slice	1 slice (12 gm)	225
Center Cut	1 slice (4.6 gm)	95
Hormel, Black Label	2 slices	298
Canadian Bacon	1 oz	315
Breakfast Strips, beef		
"Lean 'n Tasty" ® (*Oscar Mayer*)	1 slice	190
Breakfast Strips, pork		
"Lean 'n Tasty" ® (*Oscar Mayer*)	1 slice	190
BURGER KING. (*See entries under Fast Food.*)		

C

	Serving Size	Sodium (mgs)
CAMPBELL, CONDENSED. (*See entries under Soups, Canned.*)		
CANDIES		
Bonkers Chewy Candy		
All flavors	1 pc	0
Life Savers Candies		
Butter Creme Mint	1 pc	5
Butter Rum	1 pc	10
Butterscotch	1 pc	10
All other Life Savers flavors contain no sodium.		
Life Savers Confections		
Chocolate Covered Peanuts	14 pcs	15
Chocolate Covered Raisins	29 pcs	15
Junior Mints Candy	12 pcs	10
Milk Chocolate Stars	13 pcs	35
Pom Poms Caramel Candy	½ box	70
Sugar Babies Milk Caramel Tidbits	1 pkg	85
Sugar Daddy Milk Caramel Pop	1 pop	85
Life Savers Lollipops		
Assorted Flavors/Swirled Flavors	1 pc	10
Pearson's Candies/Candy Bars		
Baby Ruth	4 pcs	60
Butterfinger	4 pcs	60

	Serving Size	Sodium (mgs)
Carmel Nip Candy	4 pcs	70
Charleston Chew		
Chocolate	½ bar	40
Strawberry	½ bar	40
Vanilla	½ bar	40
Chocolate Parfait	4 pcs	70
Coffee Nip Candy	4 pcs	70
Coffioca Parfait	4 pcs	70
Licorice Nip Candy	4 pcs	70
Mint Parfait	4 pcs	70
Peanut Butter Parfait	4 pcs	70
CASSEROLES (*Pillsbury*)		
Microwave Classic Casseroles		
Beef	1 pkg	1030
Chicken	1 pkg	980
Turkey	1 pkg	840
CEREALS		
General Mills		
BooBerry	1 c	270
Bran Muffin Crisp	1 c	310
Brown Sugar and Honey Body		
Buddies	1 c	250
Cheerios	1 c	350
Cinnamon Toast Crunch	1 c	280
Cocoa Puffs	1 c	260
Count Chocula	1 c	270
Country Corn Flakes	1 c	370
Ice Cream Cones, Chocolate Chip	1 c	240
Ice Cream Cones, Vanilla	1 c	230
Crispy Wheat 'n Raisins	1 c	240
Fiber One	1 c	290
Frankenberry	1 c	270
Golden Grahams	1 c	370
Honey Buc'Wheat Crisp	1 c	320

	Serving Size	Sodium (mgs)
Honey Nut Cheerios	1 c	320
Kaboom	1 c	350
Kix	1 c	350
Lucky Charms	1 c	240
Pac-Man	1 c	260
Raisin Nut Bran	1 c	200
Rocky Road	1 c	170
S'Mores Crunch	1 c	310
Total	1 c	340
Total Corn Flakes	1 c	370
Trix	1 c	230
Wheaties	1 c	330
Hot Cereals		
Instant Total Oatmeal		
Apple Cinnamon	1¼ oz	200
Cinnamon Raisin Almond	1½ oz	180
Mixed Nut	1.3 oz	190
Quick Total Oatmeal	1 oz	70
Nature Valley Granola		
Cinnamon & Raisin	1 oz	150
Coconut & Honey	1 oz	95
Fruit & Nut	1 oz	140
Toasted Oat Mixture	1 oz	150
Heartland Natural Cereals		
Plain Variety	1 oz	80
Coconut Variety	1 oz	80
Raisin Variety	1 oz	80
Trail Mix	1 oz	80
Nabisco		
Cream of Wheat		
Apples, Raisins, and Spice	1 oz	30
Cream of Rice	1 oz	30
Instant Cream of Wheat	1 oz	30
Regular Cream of Wheat	1 oz	30

	Serving Size	Sodium (mgs)
Maple Brown Sugar, Artificially Flavored	1 oz	30
Mix 'n Eat Cream of Wheat*		
Apple and Cinnamon	1¼ oz	270
Brown Sugar Cinnamon	1¼ oz	210
Maple Brown Sugar	1¼ oz	210
Our Original	1¼ oz	210
Peach	1¼ oz	230
Strawberry	1¼ oz	230
Fruit Wheat†		
Apple	1 oz	75
Raisin	1 oz	65
Strawberry	1 oz	75
Shredded Wheat†		
Plain	1 biscuit	60
Spoon Size	1 oz	60
Shredded Wheat 'n Bran	1 oz	69
Toasted Wheat and Raisins†	1 oz	60
Post		
Alpha Bits	1 oz	180
C.W. Post Hearty Granola‡	1 oz	80
C.W. Post Hearty Granola with Raisins	1 oz	80
Cocoa Pebbles	1 oz	160
Fortified Oat Flakes	1 oz	250
Fruit & Fibre with Dates, Raisins & Walnuts	1 oz	180
Fruit & Fibre Harvest Medley	1 oz	190
Fruit & Fibre Mountain Trail	1 oz	180
Fruit & Fibre Tropical Fruit	1 oz	180

*Cereal plus 2 oz whole milk
†Cereal plus ½ c whole milk, but sodium content same if skim milk used.
‡Without milk. Add 60 mgs sodium per serving with ½ c whole milk.

	Serving Size	Sodium (mgs)
Fruity Pebbles	1 oz	150
Grape-Nuts Brand Cereal	1 oz	190
Grape-Nuts Flakes	1 oz	160
Honeycomb	1 oz	160
Natural Bran Flakes	1 oz	230
Natural Raisin Bran	1 oz	180
Post Toasties Corn Flakes	1 oz	280
Raisin Grape Nuts	1 oz	140
Smurf Berry Crunch	1 oz	75
Sugar Golden Crisp	1 oz	45
Quaker		
Quaker Oats*		
Instant Quaker Oats		
Fruit & Cream—Peaches and Cream	1 packet	190
Fruit & Cream—Strawberries and Cream	1 packet	220
Bran & Raisins	1 packet	340
Cinnamon & Spice	1 packet	360
Real Honey & Graham	1 packet	320
Regular Flavor	1 packet	400
with Artificial Maple and Brown Sugar Flavors	1 packet	330
with Raisins, Dates & Walnuts	1 packet	220
Quaker Oat Bran Cereal	⅓ c	0
Quaker Quick and Old Fashioned	⅓ c	0
Quaker Quick Creamy Wheat Farina	2½ tbs	0
Quaker Whole Wheat Hot Natural Cereal	⅓ c	0
Quaker Ready-to-Eat Cereals		

*All the above values are for uncooked cereals, and serving sizes are uncooked portions.

	Serving Size	Sodium (mgs)
Cap'n Crunch	¾ c	200
Cap'n Crunch with Crunchberries	¾ c	200
Cap'n Crunch's Peanut Butter Crunch Cereal	¾ c	250
Cinnamon Life	⅔ c	180
Halfsies	1 c	240
King Vitamin	1¼ c	280
Life	⅔ c	180
Mr. T	¾ c	230
Quaker Corn Bran Cereal	⅔ c	300
Quaker 100% Natural	¼ c	15
Quaker 100% Natural—Apple & Cinnamon	¼ c	20
Quaker 100% Natural—Raisin & Date	¼ c	10
Quaker Puffed Rice	1 c	0
Quaker Puffed Wheat	1 c	0
Quaker Shredded Wheat	2 biscuits	0
CHEESECAKE (*Jell-O*)	⅛ 8″ cake	250
CHEESE FOODS (*Nabisco*)		
Easy Cheese—Pasteurized Process Cheese Spread		
American	1 oz	350
Cheddar	1 oz	370
Cheese 'n Bacon	1 oz	350
Nacho	1 oz	340
Sharp Cheddar	1 oz	320
CHICKEN		
Breast, chunk	6¾ oz	855
Dark, chunk	6¾ oz	933
White and dark, chunk	6¾ oz	857
White and dark (Hormel), no salt	6¾ oz	75
CHINESE MEALS. (*See entries for Chun King and La Choy.*)		

	Serving Size	Sodium (mgs)
CHILI		
Hormel		
Chili Beans in Sauce	5 oz	453
Chili No Beans (10½ oz)	10½ oz	1384
Chili No Beans (25 oz)	7½ oz	1012
Chili No Beans (40 oz)	8⅓ oz	1070
Chili With Beans (15 oz)	7½ oz	855
Chili With Beans (25 oz)	8⅓ oz	1202
Chili With Beans (20 oz)	8 oz	1135
Quaker (*Van Camp's*)		
Chilee Weenee	1 c	1060
Chili With Beans	1 c	1220
Chili Without Beans	1 c	1500
Quaker (*Wolf Brand*)		
Chili With Beans	1 c	1010
Chili Without Beans	1 c	1040
Chili Without Beans Extra Spicy	scant c	960
Chili With Beans Extra Spicy	scant c	930
Chili-Mac	scant c	850
CHOCOLATE (*Baker's*)		
German's Sweet Chocolate	1 oz	0
Semi-Sweet Chocolate	1 oz	0
Semi-Sweet Chocolate Flavored Chips	¼ c	25
Semi-Sweet Real Chocolate Chips	¼ c	0
Unsweetened Chocolate	1 oz	0
CHOW MEINS. (*See entries under La Choy.*)		
CHUN KING PRODUCTS		
Divider Pak Entrées, Canned*		
Beef Chow Mein†	7 oz	560

*Values were determined with liquid drained from vegetables per package instructions.
†48-oz package containing 4 servings per package

26

	Serving Size	Sodium (mgs)
Beef Chow Mein‡	8 oz	640
Beef Pepper Oriental†	7 oz	880
Chicken Chow Mein†	7 oz	820
Chicken Chow Mein‡	8 oz	940
Shrimp Chow Mein†	7 oz	260
Stir-Fry Entrées, Canned		
Chow Mein With Beef	6 oz	540
Chow Mein With Chicken	6 oz	540
Egg Foo Young	5 oz	520
Pepper Steak	6 oz	1000
Sukiyaki	6 oz	400
Rice Mix	0.25 oz	310
Sauce/Glaze Mix for Sweet 'n Sour Entrées	3.8 oz	40
Vegetables, Sauces		
Bamboo Shoots, drained	2 oz	0
Bean Sprouts, drained	4 oz	5
Chow Mein Vegetables, drained	4 oz	20
Mustard, Brown	1 tsp	65
Soy Sauce	1 tsp	430
Sweet/Sour Sauce	1.8 oz	240
Water Chestnuts (whole or sliced), drained	2 oz	15
COCOA (*Swiss Miss Hot Cocoa Mixes—Beatrice/Hunt-Wesson*)		
Double Rich	1 envelope	160
Milk Chocolate	1 envelope	170
With Mini Marshmallows	1 envelope	150
Sugar-Free and Lite Hot Cocoa Mixes (*Swiss Miss*)		
Lite	1 envelope	160

†48-oz package containing 4 servings per package
‡24-oz package containing 2 servings per package

	Serving Size	Sodium (mgs)
Milk Chocolate	1 envelope	190
With Sugar Free Mini Marshmallows	1 envelope	190
COCONUT (*Baker's*)		
Angel Flake (bag)	⅓ c	75
Angel Flake (can)	⅓ c	5
Premium Shred	⅓ c	85
COFFEE (*General Foods International*)*†		
Cafe Amaretto	6 fl oz	25(20)
Cafe Francais	6 fl oz	25(15)
Cafe Irish Creme	6 fl oz	20
Cafe Vienna	6 fl oz	105(95)
Double Dutch Chocolate	6 fl oz	15
Irish Mocha Mint	6 fl oz	20(20)
Orange Cappuccino	6 fl oz	105(60)
Suisse Mocha	6 fl oz	25(20)
COFFEE CAKE MIXES (*Pillsbury*)		
Apple Cinnamon	⅛ cake	140
COFFEE CREAMER (*Swiss Miss Rich*)	1 tsp	5
COOKIE MIXES		
Big Batch (*General Mills*)		
Chocolate Chip‡	2 cookies	100
Sugar	2 cookies	95
Pillsbury		
Chocolate Chip	3 cookies	150
Fudge Brownies	1 bar	115
Oatmeal Raisin	3 cookies	190
Peanut Butter	3 cookies	190
Sugar	3 cookies	190

*Without whole milk. Add 60 mgs sodium per ½ c whole milk.
†Sodium values in parentheses are for Sugar Free International Coffees.
‡Mix plus ¼ cup oil and 1 egg

	Serving Size	Sodium (mgs)
COOKIES (*Nabisco*)		
Almost Home Family Style Cookies		
Fudge Chocolate Chip	2 pcs	130
Fudge Chocolate Chip Raisin	2 pcs	85
Fudge Peanut Butter Chip	2 pcs	100
Fudge 'n Vanilla Creme Sandwiches	1 pc	110
Fudge 'n Nut Brownies	1 pc	75
Iced Dutch Apple Fruit Sticks	1 pc	40
Oatmeal Chocolate Chip	2 pcs	90
Oatmeal Raisin	2 pcs	100
Old Fashioned Sugar	2 pcs	150
Peanut Butter Chocolate Chip	2 pcs	100
Peanut Butter Fudge	2 pcs	90
Real Chocolate Chip	2 pcs	100
Apple Newtons Cookies	1 pc	45
Bakers Bonus Oatmeal	2 pcs	90
Barnum's Animal Crackers	11 pcs	120
Biscos Sugar Wafers	8 pcs	35
Biscos Waffle Cremes	3 pcs	30
Blueberry Newtons	1 pc	80
Brown Edge Wafers	5 pcs	80
Bugs Bunny Graham Crackers	9 pcs	130
Cameo Creme Sandwich	2 pcs	80
Cherry Newtons	1 pc	80
Chewy Chips Ahoy! Chocolate Chip Cookies	2 pcs	110
Chips Ahoy! Pure Chocolate Chip Cookies	3 pcs	95
Chips 'n More		
Original Chocolate Chip	2 pcs	70
Coconut Chocolate Chip	2 pcs	95
Fudge Chocolate Chip	3 pcs	90
Chocolate Chip Snaps	6 pcs	100

	Serving Size	Sodium (mgs)
Chocolate Grahams	3 pcs	70
Chocolate Snaps	7 pcs	140
Cookie Break Vanilla Artificially Flavored Creme Sandwich	3 pcs	20
Cookies 'n Fudge!		
Party Grahams	3 pcs	100
Striped Chocolate Chip	3 pcs	80
Striped Wafers	3 pcs	110
Devil's Food Cakes	1 pc	70
Famous Chocolate Wafers	5 pcs	200
Famous Cookie Assortment		
Baronet Creme Sandwiches	3 pcs	75
Biscos Sugar Wafers	8 pcs	50
Butter Flavored Cookies	6 pcs	140
Cameo Creme Sandwiches	2 pcs	80
Kettle Cookies	4 pcs	115
Lorna Doone Shortbread	4 pcs	130
Oreo Chocolate Sandwich Cookies	2 pcs	170
Fig Newtons	2 pcs	100
Giggles Sandwich Cookies		
Chocolate	2 pcs	70
Vanilla	2 pcs	50
Hayday Bars—Fudge, Caramel, & Peanuts	1 bar	45
Ideal Bars—Chocolate Peanut	2 bars	130
Imported Danish Cookies	5 pcs	70
I Screams Double Dip Creme Sandwich—Chocolate	2 pcs	70
Lorna Doone Shortbread Cookies	4 pcs	130
Mallomars Chocolate Cakes	2 pcs	35
Marshmallow Puffs	1 pc	55
Marshmallow Sandwich	4 pcs	80
Marshmallow Twirls Cake	1 pc	55
Mystic Mint Sandwich Cookies	2 pcs	95

	Serving Size	Sodium (mgs)
National Arrowroot Biscuit	6 pcs	80
Nilla Wafers	7 pcs	95
Nutter Butter Real Peanut Butter Sandwich Cookies	2 pcs	100
Nutter Butter Peanut Creme Patties	4 pcs	95
Old Fashion Ginger Snaps	4 pcs	200
Oreo Big Stuf Chocolate Sandwich Cookies	1 pc	220
Oreo Chocolate Sandwich Cookies	3 pcs	170
Oreo Double Stuf Chocolate Sandwich Cookies	2 pcs	120
Oreo Fudge Covered Chocolate Sandwich Cookies	2 pcs	100
Oreo Mint Creme Chocolate Sandwich Cookies	2 pcs	160
Pantry Molasses	2 pcs	130
Pecan Shortbread Cookies	2 pcs	80
Pinwheels Chocolate & Marshmallow Cakes	1 pc	35
Pure Chocolate Middles	2 pcs	65
Social Tea Biscuits	6 pcs	105
Strawberry Newtons	1 pc	35
COOLWHIP		
CoolWhip Extra Creamy Whipped Topping	1 tbs	0
CoolWhip Non-Dairy Whipped Topping	1 tbs	0
COUGH DROPS, ALL FLAVORS		
(*Beech-nut*)	1 pc	0
COUNTRY TIME. (*See entries under Drink Mixes.*)		
CRACKERS (*Nabisco*)		
Bacon Flavored Thins	7 pcs (½ oz)	210
Better Blue Cheese Snack Thins	10 pcs (½ oz)	260

	Serving Size	Sodium (mgs)
Better Cheddars 'n Bacon Snack Thins	10 pcs (½ oz)	210
Better Cheddars Snack Thins	11 pcs (½ oz)	220
Better Nacho Snack Thins	9 pcs (½ oz)	220
Cheese Peanut Butter Sandwich	2 pcs (½ oz)	150
Cheese Ritz Crackers	5 pcs (½ oz)	120
Cheese Wheat Thins Snack Crackers	9 pcs (½ oz)	220
Cheese Tid-Bit Crackers	16 pcs (½ oz)	200
Chicken in a Biskit Flavored Crackers	7 pcs (½ oz)	115
Cinnamon Treats	2 pcs (½ oz)	80
Cracker Meal	2 tbs	0
Crown Pilot Crackers	1 pc (½ oz)	65
Dandy Soup & Oyster Crackers	20 pcs (½ oz)	220
Dip in a Chip Cheese 'n Chive Snack Crackers	8 pcs (½ oz)	130
Escort Crackers	3 pcs (½ oz)	110
Graham Cracker Crumbs	2 tbs	90
Great Crisps Baked Crispy Snacks		
Cheese 'n Chives	9 pcs (½ oz)	170
French Onion	7 pcs (½ oz)	90
Italian	9 pcs (½ oz)	200
Nacho	8 pcs (½ oz)	250
Real Bacon	9 pcs (½ oz)	230
Savory Garlic	8 pcs (½ oz)	190
Sesame	9 pcs (½ oz)	140
Sour Cream & Onion	8 pcs (½ oz)	200
Tomato & Celery	9 pcs (½ oz)	160
Holland Rusk Instant Toast	1 pc (½ oz)	35
Honey Maid Grahams	2 pcs (½ oz)	90
Malted Milk Peanut Butter Sandwich	2 pcs (½ oz)	150
Meal Mates Sesame Bread Wafers	3 pcs (½ oz)	140
Nabisco Grahams	2 pcs (½ oz)	115
Real Cheddar Cheese	13 pcs (¼ oz)	130

	Serving Size	Sodium (mgs)
Pizza	20 pcs (¼ oz)	180
Taco	14 pcs (¼ oz)	200
Nutty Wheat Thins Snack Crackers	7 pcs (¼ oz)	250
Oysterettes Soup & Oyster Crackers	18 pcs (¼ oz)	130
Premium Crackers		
Unsalted Tops	5 pcs (½ oz)	115
Saltine Crackers	5 pcs (½ oz)	180
Saltine Crackers Low Salt	5 pcs (½ oz)	115
Ritz Crackers	4 pcs (½ oz)	120
Ritz Crackers, Low Salt	4 pcs (½ oz)	60
Royal Lunch Milk Crackers	1 pc (½ oz)	80
Sea Rounds Crackers	1 pc (½ oz)	140
Sociables Crackers	6 pcs (½ oz)	130
Sultana Soda Crackers	4 pcs (½ oz)	175
Toasted Peanut Butter Sandwich	2 pcs (½ oz)	150
Triscuit Wafers	3 pcs (½ oz)	90
Triscuit Wafers, Low Salt	3 pcs (½ oz)	35
Twigs Sesame & Cheese Snack Crackers	5 pcs (½ oz)	200
Uneeda Biscuits, Unsalted Tops	3 pcs (½ oz)	100
Vegetable Thins Snack Crackers	7 pcs (½ oz)	100
Waverly Crackers	4 pcs (½ oz)	160
Wheat Thins Snack Crackers	8 pcs (½ oz)	120
Wheat Thins, Low Salt	8 pcs (½ oz)	60
Wheatsworth Stone Ground Wheat Crackers	5 pcs (½ oz)	135
Zwieback Teething Toast	2 pcs (½ oz)	20
CREAM PIES. (*See entries under Pies*)		
CUSTARD (*Jell-O*)		
Americana Golden Egg Custard Mix	½ c	140

D

	Serving Size	Sodium (mgs)
DESSERTS, FROZEN		
Jell-O		
Fruit Bars, all flavors, average values	1 bar	10
Gelatin Pops Bars, all flavors, average values	1 bar	5
Jell-O Pudding Pops Bars		
Chocolate	1 bar	80
Chocolate-Caramel Swirl	1 bar	65
Chocolate-Covered Chocolate	1 bar	75
Chocolate-Covered Vanilla	1 bar	50
Chocolate-Vanilla Swirl	1 bar	65
Chocolate with Chocolate Chips	1 bar	75
Vanilla	1 bar	50
Vanilla with Chocolate Chips	1 bar	50
Oreo Cookies 'n Cream Ice Cream		
Chocolate	3 oz	100
Mint	3 oz	100
On a Stick	1 bar	100
Sandwich	1 sandwich	300
Snackwich	1 sandwich	80
Vanilla	3 oz	100
DESSERT MIXES		
Brownies (*General Mills*)		

	Serving Size	Sodium (mgs)
Fudge Brownie Mix (regular size)*	$^1/_{16}$ mix	100
Fudge Brownie Mix (family size)	$^1/_{24}$ mix	95
Chocolate Chip	$^1/_{24}$ mix	75
Frosted	$^1/_{24}$ mix	120
German Chocolate	$^1/_{24}$ mix	110
Supreme Fudge Brownie Mix	$^1/_{24}$ mix	85
Walnut Brownie Mix (regular size)	$^1/_{24}$ mix	80
Cake Lovers Collection Cake Mixes (*General Mills*)		
Carrot (+ $^1/_{12}$ of 4 eggs and ½ c oil per serving)	$^1/_{12}$ pkg	340
Chocolate Almond (+ $^1/_{12}$ of 3 eggs and ½ c oil per serving)	$^1/_{12}$ pkg	280
Double Chocolate (+ $^1/_{12}$ of 3 eggs and ½ c oil per serving)	$^1/_{12}$ pkg	270
Dutch Apple (+ $^1/_{12}$ of 4 eggs and ⅓ c oil per serving)	$^1/_{12}$ pkg	310
Toffee Chocolate Chip (+ $^1/_{12}$ of 3 eggs and ½ c oil per serving)	$^1/_{12}$ pkg	300
Classics Dessert Mixes (*General Mills*)		
Boston Cream Pie (+ ½ egg + $^1/_6$ c milk)	$^1/_8$ pkg	390
Coconut Macaroon (no added ingredients)	$^1/_{24}$ pkg	15
Date Bar (no added sodium-containing ingredients)	$^1/_{32}$ pkg	35
Gingerbread (+ $^1/_9$ egg)	$^1/_9$ pkg	330
Golden Pound Cake (+ $^1/_6$ egg)	$^1/_{12}$ pkg	170
Lemon Chiffon Cake	$^1/_{12}$ pkg	170
Pineapple Upside-Down Cake & Topping	$^1/_{12}$ pkg	210

*Mix + ¼ c oil and 1 egg

	Serving Size	Sodium (mgs)
Pudding Cake, Chocolate	$^1/_{12}$ pkg	250
Pudding Cake, Lemon	$^1/_{12}$ pkg	270
Vienna Dream Bar (+ $^1/_4$ tsp butter & $^1/_{24}$ egg)	$^1/_{12}$ pkg	65
Creamy Frosting Mixes (*General Mills*)		
Chocolate Fudge (+ 1 tsp butter)	$^1/_{12}$ pkg	70
Coconut Almond (+ 1 tsp milk + $^1/_4$ tsp butter)	$^1/_{12}$ pkg	90
Coconut Pecan (+ $^1/_4$ tbs butter)	$^1/_{12}$ pkg	45
Cream Cheese and Nuts	$^1/_{12}$ pkg	100
Creamy Cherry (+ $^1/_4$ tbs butter)	$^1/_{12}$ pkg	90
Creamy Vanilla (+ $^1/_4$ tbs butter)	$^1/_{12}$ pkg	50
Lemon (+ $^1/_4$ tbs butter)	$^1/_{12}$ pkg	100
Milk Chocolate (+ $^1/_4$ tbs butter)	$^1/_{12}$ pkg	45
Sour Cream Chocolate Fudge (+ $^1/_4$ tbs butter)	$^1/_{12}$ pkg	80
Snackin' Cake Mixes (*General Mills*)		
Applesauce Raisin	$^1/_9$ pkg	260
Banana Walnut	$^1/_9$ pkg	260
Butter Recipe Chocolate*	$^1/_{12}$ pkg	450
Golden Chocolate Chip	$^1/_9$ pkg	260
German Chocolate Coconut Pecan	$^1/_9$ pkg	270
Golden Vanilla*	$^1/_{12}$ pkg	280
Stir 'n Frost Cake Mix With Frosting (*General Mills*)		
Chocolate Chip Cake/Chocolate Frosting	$^1/_6$ pkg	200
Chocolate-Chocolate Chip Cake/Chocolate-Chocolate Chip Frosting	$^1/_6$ pkg	260
Chocolate Devils Food Cake/Chocolate Frosting	$^1/_6$ pkg	260

* Plus $^1/_{12}$ of 3 eggs and $^1/_3$ c oil per serving

	Serving Size	Sodium (mgs)
Chocolate Fudge Cake/Vanilla Frosting	⅙ pkg	270
Spice Cake/Vanilla Frosting	⅙ pkg	310
Yellow Cake/Chocolate Frosting	⅙ pkg	210
SuperMoist Cake Mixes (*General Mills*)*		
Apple Cinnamon	1/12 pkg	280
Butter Brickle	1/12 pkg	280
Butter Pecan	1/12 pkg	280
Butter Recipe Yellow	1/12 pkg	350
Carrot	1/12 pkg	260
Cherry Chip	1/12 pkg	270
Chocolate Chip	1/12 pkg	300
Chocolate Chocolate Chip	1/12 pkg	400
Chocolate Fudge	1/12 pkg	450
Devils Food	1/12 pkg	430
German Chocolate	1/12 pkg	420
Lemon	1/12 pkg	280
Marble	1/12 pkg	300
Milk Chocolate	1/12 pkg	350
Sour Cream Chocolate	1/12 pkg	430
Sour Cream White	1/12 pkg	300
Spice	1/12 pkg	0
White	1/12 pkg	250
Yellow	1/12 pkg	300
DINNERS, FROZEN		
Armour Dinner Classics		
Beef Stroganoff	10 oz	1090
Boneless Beef Short Ribs with Barbecue Sauce	10.5 oz	1210
Chicken Fricassee	11.75 oz	1210
Chicken Milan	11.5 oz	1360

*Plus 1/12 of 3 eggs and ⅓ c oil per serving

	Serving Size	Sodium (mgs)
Chicken & Noodles in Cream Sauce	12 oz	970
Chicken with Wine and Mushroom Sauce	10.75 oz	1370
Salisbury Steak	11 oz	1300
Seafood Newburg	11.5 oz	1200
Sirloin Roast	11 oz	760
Sirloin Tips	11 oz	940
Spaghetti with Beef & Mushroom Sauce	12 oz	1500
Swedish Meatballs	12.5 oz	1730
Turkey & Dressing	11.25 oz	1370
Veal Parmigiana	13.75 oz	1260
Yankee Pot Roast	12 oz	930
Armour Dinner Classics Lite		
Baby Bay Shrimp	10.5 oz	950
Beef Pepper Steak	10.5 oz	1010
Chicken Breast Marsala	11 oz	970
Chicken Breast with Mushroom & Tomato Sauce	10 oz	970
Chicken Burgundy	10.5 oz	760
Chicken Cacciatore	11 oz	840
Chicken Oriental	10.5 oz	870
Salisbury Steak	10 oz	1000
Seafood with Natural Herbs	10.5 oz	960
Steak Diane	10 oz	770
Sweet & Sour Chicken	10.5 oz	500
Tortellini with Meat	10 oz	850
Banquet		
Boneless Chicken		
Chicken Sticks	2.6 oz	310
Chicken Breast Tenders	2.25 oz	240
Southern Fried Chicken Breast Tenders	2.25 oz	347

	Serving Size	Sodium (mgs)
Boneless Chicken Hot Bites		
Chicken & Cheddar Nuggets	2.6 oz	381
Chicken Drum Snackers	2.6 oz	389
Chicken Nuggets	2.6 oz	407
Hot 'n Spicy Chicken Nuggets	2.6 oz	356
Casseroles		
Macaroni & Cheese	8 oz	930
Spaghetti & Meat Sauce	8 oz	1242
Chicken Products		
Fried Chicken	6.4 oz	1201
Hot 'n Spicy Fried Chicken	6.4 oz	1201
Hot 'n Spicy Snacks 'n Chicken	3.75 oz	478
Fried Chicken Breast Portions	5.75 oz	707
Fried Chicken Thighs & Drumsticks	6.25 oz	781
Dinners		
Beans & Frankfurters Dinner	10 oz	1224
Chopped Beef	11 oz	598
Fried Chicken	10 oz	1095
Meat Loaf	11 oz	768
Salisbury Steak	11 oz	596
Turkey	10.5 oz	1102
Western	11 oz	716
Extra Helping Dinners		
Beef	16 oz	604
Chicken Nuggets with Barbecue Sauce	10 oz	1382
Chicken Nuggets with Sweet & Sour Sauce	10 oz	1094
Fried Chicken, all white meat	16 oz	1463
Fried Chicken	16 oz	1463
Lasagna	16.5 oz	1582
Salisbury Steak	18 oz	740
Salisbury Steak with Mushroom Gravy	18 oz	685

	Serving Size	Sodium (mgs)
Turkey	19 oz	1975
Family Favorites Dinners		
Chicken & Dumplings	10 oz	932
Macaroni & Cheese	10 oz	441
Noodles & Chicken	10 oz	455
Spaghetti & Meatballs	10 oz	575
Light & Elegant Entrées		
Beef Burgundy with Parsley Noodles	9 oz	1100
Beef Julienne with Rice & Peppers	8.5 oz	990
Beef Stroganoff with Parsley Noodles	9 oz	780
Beef Teriyaki with Rice & Pea Pods	8 oz	625
Chicken in Cheese Sauce with Rice & Broccoli	8.75 oz	800
Chicken Parmigiana with Parsley Noodles	8 oz	680
Glazed Chicken with Vegetable Rice	8 oz	660
Lasagna Florentine	11.25 oz	980
Macaroni & Cheese with Bread Crumb Topping	9 oz	1010
Shrimp Creole with Rice & Peppers	10 oz	1050
Sliced Turkey & Gravy with White & Wild Rice Stuffing	8 oz	930
Spaghetti with Meat Sauce	10.25 oz	700
Platters		
Beef	10 oz	624
Boneless Chicken Drumsticks	7 oz	682
Boneless Chicken Nuggets	6.4 oz	630
Boneless Chicken Patties	7.5 oz	753
Fish	8.75 oz	187
Ham	10 oz	1176

	Serving Size	Sodium (mgs)
All White Meat Fried Chicken	9 oz	135
All White Meat Hot 'n Spicy Fried Chicken	9 oz	135
Pot Pies		
Beef	7 oz	865
Chicken	7 oz	860
Tuna	7 oz	810
Turkey	7 oz	855
Cajun Cookin' Products		
Crawfish Bisque with Rice	15 oz	1370
Crawfish Etouffée with Rice	12 oz	1110
Seafood Gumbo with Rice	17 oz	1330
Shrimp Creole with Rice	12 oz	1130
Shrimp Etouffée with Rice	12 oz	1170
Shrimp Jambalaya	12 oz	800
Stuffed Crabs	6 oz	860
Kellogg's Tyson Gourmet Selection		
Entrées		
Chicken Original		
Barbecue	3¾ oz	400
Butter-Garlic	3¾ oz	320
Italian	3¾ oz	430
Lemon-Pepper	3¾ oz	210
Teriyaki	3¾ oz	290
Entrées		
à L'Orange	8¼ oz	440
Cacciatore	10½ oz	770
Cannelloni	11½ oz	850
Dijon	9 oz	920
Fiesta	10½ oz	1510
Francais	8¾ oz	940
Jambalaya	12¼ oz	1040
Kiev	9¼ oz	1020
Marsala	10½ oz	760

	Serving Size	Sodium (mgs)
Mesquite	9½ oz	700
Parmigiana	12¾ oz	1100
Peking	9¾ oz	950
Oriental	10¼ oz	1050
Sweet & Sour	11 oz	840
Morton		
Beef Meat Pie	1 pie	630
Chicken Meat Pie	1 pie	738
Turkey Meat Pie	1 pie	740
Swanson		
Chicken Duet Entrées		
Creamy Broccoli	6 oz	630
Creamy Green Bean	6 oz	600
Saucy Tomato	6 oz	600
Savory Wild Rice	6 oz	610
Chicken Gourmet Nuggets		
Ham and Cheese	3 oz	410
Mexican Style	3 oz	410
Pizza Style	3 oz	440
Spinach and Herb	3 oz	420
Dipsters		
Barbecue	3 oz	300
Coconola	3 oz	140
Herb	3 oz	410
Italian Style	3 oz	390
Hungry Man Dinners		
Boneless Chicken	1 complete dinner	1650
Chicken Nuggets	1 complete dinner	680
Chicken Parmigiana	1 complete dinner	2090
Chopped Beef Steak	1 complete dinner	1530

	Serving Size	Sodium (mgs)
Fried Chicken, Breast Portions	1 complete dinner	2210
Fried Chicken, Dark Portions	1 complete dinner	1780
Fish 'n Chips	1 complete dinner	1400
Lasagna	1 complete dinner	1520
Mexican Style	1 complete dinner	2050
Salisbury Steak	1 complete dinner	1620
Sliced Beef	1 complete dinner	1080
Turkey	1 complete dinner	1840
Veal Parmigiana	1 complete dinner	1760
Western Style	1 complete dinner	1730
Hungry Man Entrées		
Fried Chicken, Breast Portions	1 complete entrée	1760
Fried Chicken, Dark Portions	1 complete entrée	1380
Lasagna with Meat	1 complete entrée	1310
Salisbury Steak	1 complete entrée	1310
Sliced Beef	1 complete entrée	1040
Turkey	1 complete entrée	1650

	Serving Size	Sodium (mgs)
Le Menu Dinners		
Beef Stroganoff	1 complete dinner	1100
Breast of Chicken Parmigiana	1 complete dinner	860
Chicken à la King	1 complete dinner	1010
Chicken Cordon Bleu	1 complete dinner	860
Chicken Florentine	1 complete dinner	910
Chopped Sirloin Beef	1 complete dinner	1020
Ham Steak	1 complete dinner	1410
Pepper Steak	1 complete dinner	1100
Sirloin Beef Tips	1 complete dinner	820
Sliced Breast of Turkey with Mushrooms	1 complete dinner	1110
Stuffed Flounder	1 complete dinner	970
Sweet and Sour Chicken	1 complete dinner	950
Vegetable Lasagne	1 complete dinner	1050
Yankee Pot Roast	1 complete dinner	780
Le Menu Entrées		
Beef Burgundy	7½ oz	660
Chicken Kiev	8 oz	780
Manicotti	8½ oz	910
Oriental Chicken	8½ oz	780

	Serving Size	Sodium (mgs)
Light Style Dinners		
Beef À L'Orange	8½ oz	580
Chicken Cacciatore	8½ oz	600
Flounder Vin Blanc	8½ oz	640
Glazed Chicken Breast	8½ oz	730
3-Cheese Stuffed Shells	8½ oz	720
Turkey Divan	8½ oz	810
L'Orient Dinners		
Beef and Broccoli	8½ oz	940
Cantonese Chicken Chow Mein	8½ oz	1040
Firecracker Chicken	8½ oz	1020
Lemon Chicken	8½ oz	770
Orange Beef	8½ oz	1030
Rock Sugar Glazed Pork	8½ oz	870
Main Course Entrées		
Chicken Nibbles (edible portion only)	1 complete entrée	450
Fish 'n Fries	1 complete dinner	780
Fried Chicken (edible portion only)	1 complete dinner	630
Lasagna with Meat	1 complete dinner	1120
Macaroni and Cheese	1 complete dinner	1870
Swedish Meatballs	1 complete dinner	970
Turkey	1 complete dinner	1030
Veal Parmigiana	1 complete dinner	880
Plump & Juicy Chicken (edible portions only)		
Chicken Cutlets	3 oz	370
Chicken Dipsters	3 oz	390

	Serving Size	Sodium (mgs)
Chicken Drumlets	3 oz	370
Chicken Nibbles	3¼ oz	640
Extra Crispy Fried Chicken	3 oz	320
Fried Chicken, Breast Pieces	4½ oz	790
Fried Chicken, Assorted Pieces	3¼ oz	580
Take-Out Fried Chicken, Assorted Pieces	3¼ oz	640
Thighs and Drumsticks	3¼ oz	620
Pot Pies		
Beef	1 complete pie	760
Chicken	1 complete pie	820
Macaroni and Cheese	1 complete pie	880
Turkey	1 complete pie	780
Pot Pies, Chunky		
Chunky Beef	1 complete pie	920
Chunky Chicken	1 complete pie	850
Chunky Turkey	1 complete pie	960
3-Compartment Frozen Dinners	All values	
Beans and Franks	are for 1	1010
Beef	complete	850
Beef in Barbecue Sauce	dinner	890
Beef Enchiladas		1140
Chicken Drumlet		730
Chicken in Barbecue Sauce		1040
Chicken Nugget Platter		710
Chopped Sirloin Beef		800
Fried Chicken, Barbecue Flavor		1220

	Serving Size	Sodium (mgs)
Fried Chicken, Dark Portions		1030
Fried Chicken, White Meat		1330
Fish 'n Chips		970
Loin of Pork		770
Macaroni and Beef		880
Macaroni and Cheese		990
Meat Loaf		1010
Mexican Style Combination		1390
Noodles and Chicken		840
Polynesian Style		1430
Salisbury Steak		880
Spaghetti and Meatballs		1010
Sweet 'n Sour Chicken		480
Swiss-Steak		990
Turkey		1110
Veal Parmigiana		1060
Western Style		990
Van de Kamp's		
Green Giant Frozen Entrées		
Chicken & Broccoli	1 pkg	890
Lasagna (12 oz)	1 pkg	1660
Lasagna (18 oz)	1 pkg	2490
Macaroni & Cheese	1 pkg	1120
Mexican Classic Entrées		
Beef Tostada Supreme	8½ oz	900
Cheese Enchilada Ranchero	5½ oz	540
Crispy Fried Burrito	6 oz	825
Guacamole Packet	1½ oz	590
Shredded Beef Enchilada	5½ oz	930
Shredded Beef Taquitos with Guacamole	8 oz	990
Sirloin Burrito Grande	11 oz	1120
Mexican Holiday Enchiladas		
Beef	7½ oz	1200

	Serving Size	Sodium (mgs)
Beef Dinner	12 oz	2175
Cheese	7¼ oz	965
Cheese Dinner	12 oz	1665
Chicken	7½ oz	1105
Four Beef	8½ oz	1480
Four Cheese	8½ oz	1175
Mexican Style Dinner	11½ oz	1040

DRINK MIXES

Country Time

Lemon-Lime	8 fl oz	20
Lemonade/Pink Lemonade	8 fl oz	20
Sugar Free Lemon-Lime Lemonade/		
Pink Lemonade	8 fl oz	0

Crystal Light

All Crystal Light products are
sodium-free.

Kool-Aid

Soft Drink Mix (unsweetened)

Black Cherry, Cherry, Grape,		
Lemon-Lime, Orange	8 fl oz	0
Lemonade, Pink Lemonade	8 fl oz	0
Mountain Berry Punch	8 fl oz	15
Rainbow Punch, Sunshine Punch	8 fl oz	0
Raspberry	8 fl oz	25
Strawberry	8 fl oz	35
Strawberry Falls Punch	8 fl oz	0
Tropical Punch	8 fl oz	10

Soft Drink Mix (sugar sweetened)

Cherry	8 fl oz	0
Grape	8 fl oz	25
Lemonade	8 fl oz	0
Mountain Berry Punch	8 fl oz	15
Orange	8 fl oz	0
Pink Lemonade	8 fl oz	0

	Serving Size	Sodium (mgs)
Rainbow Punch	8 fl oz	20
Raspberry	8 fl oz	25
Strawberry, Strawberry Falls Punch	8 fl oz	0
Sunshine Punch	8 fl oz	0
Tropical Punch	8 fl oz	0
Sugar Free Diet Soft Drink Mix*		
Cherry	8 fl oz	0
Lemonade	8 fl oz	0
Mountain Berry Punch	8 fl oz	35
Orange	8 fl oz	0
Rainbow Punch	8 fl oz	0
Raspberry	8 fl oz	25
Strawberry	8 fl oz	0
Strawberry Falls Punch	8 fl oz	0
Sunshine Punch	8 fl oz	0
Tropical Punch	8 fl oz	10
Tang		
Breakfast Beverage Crystals	6 fl oz	0
Sugar Free Breakfast Crystals	6 fl oz	0
D-ZERTA PRODUCTS		
Reduced Calorie Pudding*		
Butterscotch	½ c	65
Chocolate	½ c	70
Vanilla	½ c	65
Low Calorie Gelatin (all flavors)* †	½ c	0
Reduced Calorie Whipped Topping Mix	1 tbs	5
EGG ROLLS. (*See entries under La Choy.*)		

*Sweetened with Nutrasweet
†Sodium value for gelatin does not include sodium in water used in preparation. Local water supplies vary in sodium content.

F

	Serving Size	Sodium (mgs)
FAST FOOD		
Burger King		
Whopper Sandwich		
Beef		68
Bun		399
Tomato		1
Lettuce		2
Mayonnaise		107
Ketchup		183
Pickles		119
Onion		1
SUBTOTAL		880
Cheese (optional)		284
TOTAL WITH CHEESE		1164
Hamburger/Cheeseburger		
Beef		34
Bun		263
Ketchup		121
Pickles		60
Mustard		31
TOTAL HAMBURGER		509
Cheese		142
TOTAL CHEESEBURGER		651

	Serving Size	Sodium (mgs)
Bacon Double Cheeseburger		
Beef		68
Bun		263
Cheese		284
Bacon		113
TOTAL		728
Whaler Fish Sandwich		
Fish		128
Bun		263
Tartar Sauce		202
Lettuce		1
TOTAL		594
Whopper Jr. Sandwich		
Bun		263
Beef		34
Tomato		1
Lettuce		1
Pickles		60
Ketchup		91
Mayonnaise		38
SUBTOTAL		486
Cheese (optional)		142
TOTAL WITH CHEESE		628
Ham and Cheese Specialty Sandwich		
Bun		467
Ham		710
Tomato		1
Cheese		284
Lettuce		1
Mayonnaise		71
TOTAL		1534
Chicken Specialty Sandwich		
Chicken		813
Bun		467

	Serving Size	Sodium (mgs)
Mayonnaise		142
Lettuce		1
TOTAL		1432
Chicken Tenders (6 pieces)		636
Onion Rings		665
French Fries (regular)		160
Breakfast Croissan'wich		
Egg Mix		198
Croissant		297
Cheese		142
SUBTOTAL		637
TOTAL WITH BACON		762
TOTAL WITH SAUSAGE		1042
Scrambled Egg Platter		
Egg Mix		317
Croissant		298
Hash Browns		193
SUBTOTAL		808
TOTAL WITH BACON		975
TOTAL WITH SAUSAGE		1213
French Toast Sticks		498
Great Danish		288
Milk		
2% low fat		122
Whole		119
Shakes (Medium)		
Chocolate		202
Chocolate (syrup added)		225
Vanilla		205
Vanilla (syrup added)		213
Soft Drinks		
Pepsi-Cola		depends
Diet Pepsi		on the
7-Up		water supply

	Serving Size	Sodium (mgs)
Desserts		
Apple Pie		412
Salad Bar		
Salad (typical without dressing		23
Salad Dressing*		
Bleu Cheese		309
House		260
Reduced Calorie Italian		426
Thousand Island		228
McDonald's		
Breakfast Foods		
Apple Danish		370
Biscuit with Biscuit Spread		790
Biscuit with Egg, Bacon, and Cheese		1270
Biscuit with Sausage		1150
Biscuit with Sausage and Egg		1300
Cinnamon Raisin Danish		430
Egg McMuffin		885
English Muffin with Butter		310
Hash Brown Potatoes		325
Hot Cakes with Butter and Syrup		1070
Pork Sausage		420
Iced Cheese Danish		420
Raspberry Danish		310
Sausage McMuffin		940
Sausage McMuffin with Egg		1040
Scrambled Eggs		205
Chicken McNuggets and Sauces		
Chicken McNuggets		510
Sauces		
Barbecue		310

*Each salad dressing comes in an individual cup.

	Serving Size	Sodium (mgs)
Honey		0
Hot Mustard		260
Sweet and Sour		190
Sandwiches		
Big Mac		980
Cheeseburger		310
Filet-O-Fish		800
Hamburger		510
Mc D.L.T.		1030
Quarter Pounder		720
Quarter Pounder with Cheese		1220
Potatoes		
French Fries		110
Shakes		
Chocolate		300
Strawberry		210
Vanilla		200
Desserts		
Apple Pie		86
Chocolate Chip Cookies		310
Hot Caramel Sundae		145
Hot Fudge Sundae		170
McDonaldland Cookies		360
Soft Serve and Cones		110
Strawberry Sundae		90
Milks and Juices		
Grapefruit Juice	6 oz	0
Milk, 2% butter fat	6 oz	125
Orange Juice	6 oz	0
Skim Milk	8 oz	130
FLOURS (*Pillsbury's Best*)		
All Purpose	1 cup	0
Ballard All Purpose	1 cup	0
Bohemian Style Rye and Wheat	1 cup	0

	Serving Size	Sodium (mgs)
Bread		
Medium Rye	1 cup	0
Sauce 'n Blend	2 tbs	0
Self-Rising Bleached or Unbleached	1 cup	1290
Whole Wheat	1 cup	10

FRANCO AMERICAN CANNED PRODUCTS (*Campbell's*)

	Serving Size	Sodium (mgs)
Au Jus Gravy	2 oz	290
Beef Gravy	2 oz	310
Beef Ravioli in Meat Sauce	7½ oz	1090
Beef RavioliO's in Meat Sauce	7½ oz	900
Brown Gravy with Onions	2 oz	340
Chicken Giblet Gravy	2 oz	300
Chicken Gravy	2 oz	310
Macaroni & Cheese	7⅜ oz	960
Mushroom Gravy	2 oz	310
PizzO's	7½ oz	1060
Pork Gravy	2 oz	350
Spaghetti in Tomato Sauce with Cheese	7⅜ oz	810
Spaghetti with Meatballs in Tomato Sauce	7⅜ oz	830
SpaghettiO's in Tomato & Cheese Sauce	7⅜ oz	910
SpaghettiO's with Sliced Beef Franks in Tomato Sauce	7⅜ oz	970
Turkey Gravy	2 oz	290

FROSTINGS, READY TO SPREAD
Creamy Deluxe Ready-to-Spread Frostings (*General Mills*)

	Serving Size	Sodium (mgs)
Amaretta	1/12 tub	90
Butter Pecan	1/12 tub	90
Caramel Chocolate Nut	1/12 tub	60
Caramel Chocolate Nut Minimorsels	1/12 tub	60

	Serving Size	Sodium (mgs)
Cherry	$1/_{12}$ tub	100
Chocolate	$1/_{12}$ tub	100
Double Chocolate Chip Minimorsels	$1/_{12}$ tub	85
Lemon	$1/_{12}$ tub	100
Orange	$1/_{12}$ tub	90
Rainbow Chip Minimorsels	$1/_{12}$ tub	90
Rocky Road Minimorsels	$1/_{12}$ tub	80
Sour Cream White	$1/_{12}$ tub	100
Vanilla	$1/_{12}$ tub	100

FROZEN FOODS. (*See entries under Pancake Mixes.*)

FRUIT SNACKS (*Del Monte*)

	Serving Size	Sodium (mgs)
Pineapple Nuggets	0.9 oz	25
Sierra Trail Mix	0.9 oz	35
Tropical Fruit Mix	0.9 oz	15
Yogurt Raisins	0.9 oz	25
Yogurt Raisins, Strawberry	0.9 oz	20

G

	Serving Size	Sodium (mgs)
GELATIN*		
Jell-O		
Regular		
Blackberry	½ c	35
Cherry	½ c	70
Concord Grape	½ c	35
Lemon	½ c	75
Lime	½ c	55
Orange-Pineapple	½ c	65
Wild Raspberry	½ c	75
All other flavors	½ c	50
Sugar Free		
Cherry	½ c	80
Lemon	½ c	55
Lime	½ c	60
Strawberry	½ c	65
All other flavors	½ c	50
Royal		
Regular		
Apple	½ c	95
Blueberry	½ c	95
Cherry	½ c	95

*Does not include sodium content in added water.

	Serving Size	Sodium (mgs)
Lemon	½ c	100
Lemon-Lime	½ c	95
Lime	½ c	90
Orange	½ c	95
Peach	½ c	100
Pineapple	½ c	90
Raspberry	½ c	95
Strawberry	½ c	100
Strawberry Banana	½ c	95
Tropical Fruit	½ c	95
Sugar Free Gelatins		
Cherry	½ c	70
Lime	½ c	75
Orange	½ c	70
Raspberry	½ c	70
Strawberry	½ c	70

GOOD SEASONS SALAD DRESSING MIX. (*See entries under Salad Dressings*)

GRANOLA BARS

General Mills Nature Valley

Almond	1 bar	85
Chocolate Chip	1 bar	75
Cinnamon	1 bar	70
Coconut	1 bar	65
Oats 'n Honey	1 bar	65
Peanut	1 bar	80
Peanut Butter	1 bar	70

Nature Valley Dandy Bar

Chocolate Almond	1 bar	105
Dark Chocolate	1 bar	110
Milk Chocolate	1 bar	105
Peanut Butter	1 bar	110

	Serving Size	Sodium (mgs)
Quaker Oats Co.		
Chewy Raisin & Cinnamon (8 oz)	1 bar	100
Chewy Peanut Butter (8 oz)	1 bar	130
Chewy Honey & Oats (8 oz)	1 bar	110
Chewy Chocolate Chip (8 oz)	1 bar	95
Chewy Chunky Nut & Raisin (8 oz)	1 bar	95
Chewy Peanut Butter & Chocolate Chip	1 bar	120
Chewy Chocolate, Graham & Marshmallow	1 bar	110
Dipps Bars (all 6 oz)		
Honey & Oats	1 bar	80
Peanut Butter	1 bar	105
Raisin & Almond	1 bar	100
Chocolate Chip	1 bar	80
Mint Chocolate Chip	1 bar	70
Rocky Road	1 bar	70
Caramel Nut	1 bar	75
GRITS (*Quaker Instant*)		
Enriched Yellow Hominy Quick Grits	3 tbs	0
White Hominy Instant Grits	1 packet	520
with Imitation Bacon Bits	1 packet	730
with Imitation Ham Bits	1 packet	900
with Real Cheddar Cheese Flavor	1 packet	700
GUM (*Life Savers Gum Products*)		
Beech-Nut, all flavors	1 pc	0
Beechies Candy Coated, all flavors	1 pc	0
Bubble Yum	1 pc	0
Care*Free Sugarless Gum, all flavors	1 pc	0
Fruit Stripe Gum, all flavors	1 pc	0

H

	Serving Size	Sodium (mgs)
HAM		
Hormel		
Black Label (1½ lbs)	4 oz	1324
Black Label (3 lbs)	4 oz	1315
Black Label (5 lbs)	4 oz	1245
Ham Patties	1 patty	456
Ham and Cheese Patties	1 patty	468
Holiday Glazed Ham (3 lbs)	4 oz	N.A.
Deviled Ham	1 tbs	105
Ham, Chunk	6¾ oz	2241
Chopped Ham (12 oz)	2 oz	703
Chopped Ham (8 lbs)	3 oz	1062
Oscar Mayer		
Boneless, Jubilee	1 oz	370
Jubilee, Canned	1 oz	285
Slice, Jubilee	1 oz	350
Steak, Jubilee	57-gm steak	710
HORMEL. (*See entries under Chili.*)		
HOT DOGS (*Oscar Mayer*)		
Cheese Hot Dogs	1 link (45 gm)	475
Cheese Hot Dogs/Bacon & Cheddar	1 link (45 gm)	510

	Serving Size	Sodium (mgs)
Cheese Hot Dogs Nacho Style	1 link (45 gm)	550
Franks, Beef	1 link (45 gm)	460
Franks, Beef Jumbo	1 link (57 gm)	585
Franks, Beef "The Big One" ™	1 link (113 gm)	1155
Franks, Bun-Length Beef	1 link (57 gm)	585
Franks, Cheese	1 link (45 gm)	534
Wieners	1 link (45 gm)	460
Wieners, Bun-Length	1 link (57 gm)	580
Wieners, Jumbo	1 link (57 gm)	580
Wieners, Little	1 link (9 gm)	90
HUNGRY JACK. (*See entries under Biscuits.*)		
HUNT'S PRODUCTS (*Beatrice/Hunt-Wesson*)		
All Natural Barbecue Sauce		
Original	1 tbs	200
Hickory	1 tbs	200
Hot & Zesty	1 tbs	200
Onion	1 tbs	200
Crushed Tomatoes	½ c	300
Ketchup	½ oz	160
No Salt Added		
Ketchup	1 tbs	50
Tomato Paste	2 oz	25

	Serving Size	Sodium (mgs)
Tomato Sauce	4 oz	25
Spaghetti Sauce		
Traditional	4 oz	510
Meat	4 oz	520
Mushroom	4 oz	520
Stewed Tomatoes	4 oz	460
Tomato Herb Sauce	4 oz	495
Tomato Juice	6 oz	550
Tomato Paste	2 oz	150
Tomato Paste Italian Style	2 oz	525
Tomato Puree	4 oz	185
Tomato Sauce	4 oz	665
with Bits	4 oz	695
with Cheese	4 oz	795
with Mushrooms	4 oz	710
with Onions	4 oz	670
Special	4 oz	315

J

	Serving Size	Sodium (mgs)
JELL-O. (*See entries under Pudding and Pie Mix.*)		
JUICE, CANNED (*Campbell's*)		
Juice Works		
Apple	6 oz	30
Appleberry	6 oz	30
Cherry	6 oz	15
Grape	6 oz	15
Orange	6 oz	65
Strawberry	6 oz	40
Tomato	6 oz	570
V8 Vegetable Juice	6 oz	620
No-Salt-Added	6 oz	45
Spicy Hot	6 oz	620
Kool-Aid Koolers Juice Drink		
Cherry	8 oz	10
Grape	8 oz	10
Mountain Berry Punch	8 oz	10
Orange, Rainbow Punch	8 oz	10
Tropical Punch	8 oz	10
Ocean Spray		
Apple Juice	100 gm	14
Cran-Blueberry Drink	100 gm	10
Lo-Cal Cran-Raspberry Drink	100 gm	10

	Serving Size	Sodium (mgs)
Mauna La'i Guava Passion Fruit Drink	100 gm	10
Pink Grapefruit Cocktail	100 gm	15

The following Ocean Spray products have less than 10 mg of sodium per 100 grams: Cranberry Juice Cocktail, Cranapple Drink, Lo-Cal Cranapple Drink, Cran-Grape Drink, Cranicot Drink, Cran-Raspberry Drink, Cran-tastic (blended juice) drink, Grapefruit Juice, Pineapple Grapefruit Juice Cocktail, Mauna La'i Guava Fruit Drink, Orange Juice.

Tropicana

	Serving Size	Sodium (mgs)
Apple	8 oz	7
Grapefuit	8 oz	1
Orange	8 oz	1

L

	Serving Size	Sodium (mgs)
LA CHOY		
Bi-Packs		
Bamboo Shoots	¼ c drained	0
Beef Chow Mein	¾ c prepared	850
Beef Pepper Oriental	¾ c prepared	950
Chicken Chow Mein	¾ c prepared	970
Chicken Sweet & Sour	¾ c prepared	440
Pork Chow Mein	¾ c prepared	950
Shrimp Chow Main	¾ c prepared	860
Sukiyaki	¾ c prepared	740
Vegetable Chow Mein	¾ c prepared	640
Canned Vegetables		
Bean Sprouts	⅔ c drained	20
Chop Suey Vegetables	½ c drained	320
Fancy Mixed Chinese Vegetables	½ c drained	30
Chinese Fried Rice	¾ c	820
Chinese Hot Mustard	1 tsp	130
Chow Meins, Canned		
Beef	¾ c	890
Chicken	¾ c	800
Meatless	¾ c	780
Shrimp	¾ c	820
Egg Foo Young Dinner (*prepared*)	1 patty, ¼ c sauce	760

	Serving Size	Sodium (mgs)
Egg Roll Entrées		
Almond Chicken	2 rolls	1020
Beef & Broccoli	2 rolls	1060
Spicy Oriental Chicken	2 rolls	690
Sweet & Sour Pork	2 rolls	720
Egg Rolls		
Lobster (7¼-oz pkg)	3 rolls	240
Lobster (15-oz pkg)	1 roll	240
Shrimp (7¼-oz pkg)	3 rolls	210
Shrimp (15-oz pkg)	1 roll	575
Entrées, Canned		
Beef Pepper Oriental	¾ c	1060
Sweet & Sour Oriental with Chicken	¾ c	1420
Sweet & Sour Oriental with Pork	¾ c	1540
Fresh and Lite Frozen Entrées		
Beef Teriyaki	10 oz (1 pkg)	900
Sweet and Sour Chicken	10 oz (1 pkg)	860
Noodles	½ c	230
Pepper Steak (*prepared*)	¾ c	960
Ramen Noodles with Oriental Flavorings	¼ pkg	74
Rice Noodles	½ c	420
Soy Sauce	100 gm	4750
Sukiyaki Dinner (*prepared*)	¾ c	990
Sweet and Sour (*prepared*)	¾ c	1210
Sweet and Sour Sauce	1 tbs	320
Teriyaki Marinade and Sauce	1 oz	1640
LIFE SAVERS CANDIES. (*See entries under Candies.*)		
LUNCHEON MEATS		
Bologna		
Hormel		
Beef	2 slices	592

	Serving Size	Sodium (mgs)
Meat	2 slices	599
Light and Lean	2 slices	0
Oscar Mayer		
Beef	1 slice (28 gm)	300
Garlic Beef	1 slice (28 gm)	295
Garlic Beef with Cheese	1 slice (28 gm)	240
Plain	1 slice (28 gm)	300
Wisconsin Made Ring	1 slice (28 gm)	235
Braunschweiger (*Oscar Mayer*)		
German Brand (tube)	28 gm (1 oz)	345
Liver Sausage (sliced)	1 slice (28 gm)	325
Liver Sausage (tube)	28 gm (1 oz)	320
Breast of Turkey (*Hormel*)	2 slices	484
Breast of Turkey, smoked (*Hormel*)	2 slices	540
Breast of Turkey (*Oscar Mayer*)	1 slice (21 gm)	265
Breast of Turkey, smoked (*Oscar Mayer*)	1 slice (21 gm)	295
Chopped Ham (*Hormel*)	2 slices	685
Chopped Ham (*Oscar Mayer*)	1 slice (28 gm)	325
Cotto Salami (*Hormel*)	2 slices	750
Cotto Salami (*Oscar Mayer*)	1 slice (23 gm)	290
Cotto Salami, beef (*Oscar Mayer*)	1 slice (23 gm)	295
Genoa Salami (*Oscar Mayer*)	1 slice (9 gm)	155

	Serving Size	Sodium (mgs)
Ham and Cheese Loaf (*Hormel*)	2 slices	668
Ham and Cheese Loaf (*Oscar Mayer*)	1 slice (28 gm)	360
Hard Salami (*Hormel*)	2 slices	339
Hard Salami (*Oscar Mayer*)	1 slice (9 gm)	165
Head Cheese (*Oscar Mayer*)	1 slice (28 gm)	340
Honey Loaf (*Hormel*)	2 slices	584
Iowa Brand Loaf (*Hormel*)	2 slices	607
Jellied Beef Loaf (*Hormel*)	2 slices	900
Lean Cold Cuts (*Oscar Mayer*)*		
Bar B-Q Loaf (90% fat free)	28 gm	345
Beef Italian Style	1 slice (17 gm)	210
Beef, smoked	1 slice (14 gm)	185
Canadian Style Bacon	1 slice (28 gm)	390
Chicken Breast, oven roasted	1 slice (28 gm)	340
Chicken Breast, smoked	1 slice (28 gm)	385
Corned Beef	1 slice (17 gm)	200
Corned Beef Loaf, jellied	1 slice (28 gm)	275
Ham, boiled	1 slice (21 gm)	250
Ham, cracked black pepper	1 slice (21 gm)	270
Ham with honey	1 slice (21 gm)	270

*Between 90 and 95% fat free

	Serving Size	Sodium (mgs)
Ham, Italian Style	1 slice (21 gm)	265
Ham, smoked	1 slice (21 gm)	265
Honey Loaf	1 slice (28 gm)	365
Honey Roll Sausage, beef	1 slice (23 gm)	320
Luxury Loaf	1 slice (28 gm)	300
New England Brand Sausage	1 slice (23 gm)	290
Pastrami	1 slice (17 gm)	215
Peppered Loaf	1 slice (28 gm)	360
Liver Cheese, pork fat wrapped (*Oscar Mayer*)	1 slice (38 gm)	435
Luncheon Meat (*Oscar Mayer*)	1 slice (28 gm)	340
Old-Fashioned Loaf (*Oscar Mayer*)	1 slice (28 gm)	335
Olive Loaf (*Hormel*)	2 slices	810
Olive Loaf (*Oscar Mayer*)	1 slice (28 gm)	395
Pepperoni (*Hormel*)	2 slices	281
Pickle Loaf (*Hormel*)	2 slices	752
Pickle & Pimiento Loaf (*Oscar Mayer*)	1 slice (28 gm)	395
Picnic Loaf (*Oscar Mayer*)	1 slice (28 gm)	330
Salami for Beer (*Oscar Mayer*)	1 slice (23 gm)	280

	Serving Size	Sodium (mgs)
Salami for Beer, beef (*Oscar Mayer*)	1 slice (23 gm)	280
Salami, Beef (*Hormel*)	2 slices	219
Spam Luncheon Meat (7 oz) (*Hormel*)	1¾ oz	756
Spam Luncheon Meat (12 oz) (*Hormel*)	2 oz	862
Spam, Smoke Flavored (*Hormel*)	2 oz	774
Spam with Cheese Chunks (*Hormel*)	2 oz	811
Spiced Ham (5 lb) (*Hormel*)	3 oz	1093
Spiced Luncheon Meat (*Hormel*)	2 slices	702
Summer Sausage (*Hormel*)	2 slices	706
Summer Sausage (*Oscar Mayer*)	1 slice (23 gm)	330
Underwood Meat Spreads		
Deviled Ham	½ can	640
Chunky Chicken Spread	½ can	575
Roast Beef Spread	½ can	515
Liverwurst Spread	½ can	470
Corned Beef Spread	½ can	605

M

	Serving Size	Sodium (mgs)
MARGARINE		
Blue Bonnet		
Stick	1 tbs	95
Diet	1 tbs	100
Soft	1 tbs	95
Soft Whipped	1 tbs	70
Whipped	1 tbs	70
Blue Bonnet Spread (52% vegetable oil)	1 tbs	100
Blue Bonnet Spread (52% fat)	1 tbs	110
Fleischmann's		
Diet	1 tbs	100
Diet with Lite Salt	1 tbs	50
Light Corn Oil Spread Stick	1 tbs	70
Light Corn Oil Spread, soft	1 tbs	95
Stick	1 tbs	95
Squeeze	1 tbs	85
Whipped, lightly salted	1 tbs	60
Mazola		
Diet Mazola Reduced Calorie Margarine	1 tbs	130
Mazola Margarine	1 tbs	100
Mazola Margarine (No Salt)	1 tbs	0

	Serving Size	Sodium (mgs)
Mazola No Stick	0.72 gm (from 2.5 second spray)	0
Nucoa		
Nucoa Margarine	1 tbs	160
Nucoa Soft Margarine	1 tbs	150
MATZOS (*Manischewitz*)		
American Matzo Cracker	1 board	0
Daily Thin Tea Matzos	1 pc	0.61
Dietetic Matzo Thins	1 pc	0.30
Egg 'n Onion Matzos	1 pc	180
Matzo Cracker Miniatures	10–20 crackers	0
Matzo Meal	1 c	2.8
Passover Egg Matzo Crackers	10 crackers	under 5
Passover Egg Matzos	1 pc	0
Passover Matzos	1 pc	0
Unsalted Matzos	1 pc	under 5
Wheat Matzo Crackers	10 crackers	under 10
Wheat Meal Matzos with Bran	1 pc	under 5
MAYONNAISE (*Hellmann's*)	1 tbs	80
MCDONALD'S. (*See entries under Fast Food.*)		
MEXICAN MEALS. (*See entries for Entrées, Old El Paso Products, Ortega Products.*)		
MILK, EVAPORATED		
Pet Evaporated Milk	½ c	140
Pet Evaporated Milk, Skimmed	½ c	150
MINUTE RICE. (*See entries under Rice Dishes.*)		
MOLASSES (*Brer Rabbit*)		
Light	1 tbs	10

	Serving Size	Sodium (mgs)
Dark	1 tbs	15
MRS. PAUL'S. (*See entries under Seafood, Frozen.*)		
MUFFIN MIX (*General Mills*)		
Apple Cinnamon	All values	140
Banana Mix	for $^1/_{12}$ Mix	200
Carrot Nut	+ $^1/_{12}$ egg	170
Cinnamon Streusel	and 2 tsp	210
Chocolate Chip	milk per	180
Oatmeal Chip	serving	125
Tart Cherry		140
Wild Blueberry		160

N

	Serving Size	Sodium (mgs)
NOODLES		
Manischewitz		
Egg Noodle Barley	All values	15
Egg Noodle Bows	for 2 oz	15
Egg Noodle Flakes	dry	15
Egg Noodle Toasted Barley		15
Enriched Fine Egg Noodles (7-oz pkg)		15
Enriched Fine Egg Noodles (12-oz pkg)		15
Enriched Wide Egg Noodles		15
Medium Egg Noodles (7-oz pkg)		15
Super Wide Egg Noodles		15
Vegetable Egg Noodles		15
Mueller's		
Egg Noodles		10
Golden Rich Egg Noodles		5
Lasagna		0
Tri Color Twists		20
All other pasta		0
NUTS	All values	
Fisher Dry Roasted Nuts	for 1 oz	160
Cashews		
Lightly Salted Peanuts		85

	Serving Size	Sodium (mgs)
Mixed Nuts	All values	110
Peanuts	for 1 oz	230
Sunflower Nuts		110
Unsalted Peanuts/Sunflower Nuts		0
Fisher Honey Roasted Nuts		
Almonds		75
Cashews		100
Peanuts		150
Peanut/Cashew Mix		90
Peanuts (dry roasted)		90
Fisher Oil Slightly Salted Roasted Nuts		
Cashews & Almonds		40
Mixed Nuts		40
Spanish Nuts		55
Planter's		
Almonds (Blanched, Slivered, Whole, Sliced)		0
Black Walnuts		0
English Walnuts (Whole, Halves, and Pieces)		0
Fruit 'n Nut Mix		59
Nut Topping		0
Natural Pistachios		250
Pecans (Chips, Halves, Pieces)		0
Raw Spanish Peanuts		0
Roasted-in-Shell Peanuts, Salted		160
Sunflower Seeds		30
Sweet 'n Crunchy Peanuts		20
Tavern Nuts		65
Planter's Dry Roasted Nuts		
Almonds		200
Mixed Nuts		250
Peanuts		250

	Serving Size	Sodium (mgs)
Pistachios	All values	250
Roasted Cashews	for 1 oz	210
Sesame Nut Mix		330
Spanish Peanuts		200
Sunflower Nuts		260
Unsalted Cashews		0
Planter's Honey Roasted Nuts		
Almonds		180
Cashews		170
Cashews & Peanuts		170
Dry Roasted Peanuts		90
Peanuts		180
Planter's Oil Roasted Nuts		
Cashew Halves		135
Cocktail Peanuts		160
Deluxe Mixed Nuts		135
Fancy Cashews		135
Mixed Nuts		130
Redskin Peanuts		150
Salted Peanuts		160
Sesame Nut Mix		220
Spanish Peanuts		150
Sunflower Nuts		130

O

	Serving Size	Sodium (mgs)
OCEAN SPRAY. (*See entries under Sauces.*)		
OIL		
Mazola Corn Oil	1 tbs	0
Planter's Peanut Oil	1 tbs	0
Planter's Popcorn Oil	1 tbs	0
Wesson Corn, Sunflower, Vegetable Oils	1 tbs	0
OLD EL PASO PRODUCTS		
Beef Enchiladas	2 enchiladas	431
Chili Con Carne	1 c	907
Chili with Beans	1 c	1037
Corn Tortillas	1 tortilla	140
Enchilada Sauce, hot	¼ c	248
Enchilada Sauce, mild	¼ c	250
Flour Tortillas	1 tortilla	360
Garbanzo Beans	½ c	247
Green Chili Enchilada Sauce	¼ c	400
Green Chilies, chopped	2 tbs	69
Green Chilies, whole	1 chili	105
Hot Mexican Rice	½ c	390
Hot Picante Sauce (16-oz jar)	2 tbs	310
Hot Taco Sauce	2 tbs	131
Jalapeño, whole	2 peppers	478

	Serving Size	Sodium (mgs)
Medium Picante Sauce (16-oz jar)	2 tbs	310
Mild Picante Sauce	2 tbs	330
Mexican Crisps	5 crisps	75
Mild Mexican Rice	½ c	370
Mild Picante Sauce (16-oz jar)	2 tbs	310
Mild Taco Sauce	2 tbs	126
Mini Taco Shells	1 shell	20
Nachips	10 chips	111
Picante Salsa	2 tbs	163
Refried Beans	¼ c	400
with Green Chilies	¼ c	400
with Sausage	½ c	300
Super Size Taco Shells	1 shell	90
Taco Seasoning	1 pkg	3569
Taco Shell	1 shell	47
Tamales	2 tamales	378
Thick 'n Chunky Salsa	2 tbs	167
Tomatoes and Green Chilies	¼ c	273
Tostado Shells	1 shell	110

ORTEGA PRODUCTS

	Serving Size	Sodium (mgs)
Acapulco Dip	1 oz	0
Enchilada Salsa, mild	1 oz	280
Enchilada Salsa, hot	1 oz	280
Green Chilies (whole, diced, strips, sliced)	1 oz	20
Green Chili Salsa, mild	1 oz	180
Green Chili Salsa, medium	1 oz	180
Green Chili Salsa, hot	1 oz	180
Hot Peppers (whole, diced)	1 oz	0
Jalapeño Peppers (whole, diced)	1 oz	20
Mild Taco Meat Seasoning	1 oz	1970
Mild Taco Meat Seasoning (prepared with 1 lb ground beef & 1½ c water)	1 oz	105

	Serving Size	Sodium (mgs)
Picante Salsa	1 oz	300
Ranchero Salsa	1 oz	250
Taco Salsa, mild	1 oz	290
Taco Salsa, hot	1 oz	300
Taco Sauce, mild	1 oz	220
Taco Sauce, hot	1 oz	210
Taco/Tostado Shells	1 shell	5
Tomatoes & Jalapeños	1 oz	120
Western Style Taco Sauce	1 oz	180

OSCAR MAYER. (*See entries under Ham, Luncheon Meats.*)

P

	Serving Size	Sodium (mgs)
PANCAKE MIXES		
Aunt Jemima Products		
Frozen Foods		
Apple Cinnamon Waffles	2 waffles	630
Blueberry Pancakes	3 4″ pan-cakes	1030
Blueberry Waffles	2 waffles	630
Buttermilk Pancakes	3 4″ pan-cakes	1020
Buttermilk Waffles	2 waffles	700
Cinnamon Swirl French Toast	2 slices	560
Original Flavor Pancakes	3 4″ pan-cakes	1010
Original Waffles	2 waffles	650
Pancake Batter	3 4″ pan-cakes	1110
Raisin French Toast	2 slices	550
Raisin Waffles	2 waffles	680
Mixes and Flours		
Bolted White Corn Meal Mix	$\frac{1}{6}$ c	460
Bolted Yellow Corn Meal Mix	$\frac{1}{6}$ c	460
Buckwheat Pancake and Waffle Mix	3 4″ pan-cakes	520

	Serving Size	Sodium (mgs)
Buttermilk Complete Pancake & Waffle Mix	3 4″ pancakes	960
Buttermilk Pancake and Waffle Mix	3 4″ pancakes	990
Buttermilk Self-Rising White Corn Meal Mix	3 tbs	590
Complete Pancake & Waffle Mix	3 4″ pancakes	460
Easy Mix Coffee Cake	1/8 cake	270
Easy Mix Corn Bread	1/6 loaf	600
Enriched Self-Rising Flour	1/4 c	500
Enriched White Corn Meal	3 tbs	0
Enriched White Hominy Grit	3 tbs	0
Enriched Yellow Corn Meal	3 tbs	0
Lite Syrup	1 fl oz	65
The Original Pancake & Waffle Mix	3 4″ pancakes	550
Self-Rising White Corn Meal Mix	1/6 c	510
Self-Rising Enriched Bolted Corn Meal	1/6 c	520
Syrup	1 fl oz	25
Butter Lite Syrup	1 fl oz	65
Whole Wheat Pancake & Waffle Mix	3 4″ pancakes	730
Hungry Jack (*Pillsbury*)		
Blueberry	3 4″ pancakes	780
Blueberry Complete Packets	3 4″ pancakes	680
Buttermilk	3 4″ pancakes	540
Buttermilk Complete	3 4″ pancakes	710

	Serving Size	Sodium (mgs)
Extra Lights	3 4" pan-cakes	440
Extra Lights Complete	3 4" pan-cakes	700
Panshakes	3 4" pan-cakes	840
Pillsbury		
Buttermilk	3 pancakes	590
Original	3 pancakes	550
PASTRIES (*Pillsbury*)		
Apple Turnover	1 turnover	320
Blueberry Turnover	1 turnover	310
Cherry Turnover	1 turnover	310
PEANUT BUTTER		
Peter Pan		
Creamy	2 tbs	150
Crunchy	2 tbs	120
Sodium Free Creamy	2 tbs	0
Salt Free Creamy (no salt added)	2 tbs	0
Salt Free Crunchy (no salt added)	2 tbs	0
Skippy		
Creamy	1 tbs	75
Super Chunk	1 tbs	65
PEPPERIDGE FARM PRODUCTS		
Breads		
Cinnamon	2 slices	170
Cracked Wheat	2 slices	280
Dijon Rye	2 slices	490
Family Pumpernickel	2 slices	450
Honey Bran	2 slices	340
Honey Wheatberry	2 slices	290
Multi-Grain, Very Thin	2 slices	180
Oatmeal	2 slices	370
Party Dijon Slices	2 slices	190

	Serving Size	Sodium (mgs)
Party Dijon Pumpernickel Slices	2 slices	180
Party Rye Slices	2 slices	280
Raisin with Cinnamon	2 slices	170
Seeded Family Rye	2 slices	220
Seedless Rye	2 slices	420
Toasting White	2 slices	430
White Sandwich	2 slices	270
White	2 slices	270
Very Thin White	2 slices	160
Wheat	2 slices	380
Wheat Germ	2 slices	280
Whole Wheat	2 slices	230
Whole Wheat, very thin	2 slices	160
Cookies		
Biscuits, Assorted Cookies		
Champagne	2 cookies	60
Chocolate Laced Pirouettes	2 cookies	40
Original Pirouettes	2 cookies	45
Seville	2 cookies	50
Southport	2 cookies	75
Paris	2 cookies	45
Distinctive Cookies		
Bordeaux	3 cookies	65
Brussels	3 cookies	95
Brussels Mint	3 cookies	120
Cappuccino	3 cookies	50
Capri	2 cookies	95
Chessmen	3 cookies	70
Geneva	3 cookies	75
Lido	2 cookies	85
Milano	3 cookies	55
Orange Milano	3 cookies	105
Mint Milano	3 cookies	55
Nassau	2 cookies	90

	Serving Size	Sodium (mgs)
Orleans	3 cookies	35
Tahiti	2 cookies	50
Fruit Cookies		
Apricot Raspberry	3 cookies	85
Strawberry	3 cookies	70
Kitchen Hearth Cookies		
Date Nut Granola	3 cookies	100
Date Pecan	3 cookies	65
Raisin Bran	3 cookies	85
Old Fashioned Cookies		
Brownie Chocolate Nut	3 cookies	80
Chocolate Chip	3 cookies	95
Chocolate Chocolate Chip	3 cookies	70
Ginger Man	3 cookies	80
Hazelnut	3 cookies	105
Irish Oatmeal	3 cookies	125
Lemon Nut Crunch	3 cookies	80
Molasses Crisps	3 cookies	75
Oatmeal Raisin	3 cookies	170
Shortbread	3 cookies	75
Sugar	3 cookies	120
Special Collection		
Almond Supreme	2 cookies	45
Chocolate Chunk Pecan	2 cookies	50
Milk Chocolate Macadamia	2 cookies	75
Crackers		
Croutons		
Cheese & Garlic	½ oz	180
Onion & Garlic	½ oz	170
Seasoned	½ oz	200
Distinctive Crackers		
Cracked Wheat	4 crackers	200
English Water Biscuit	4 crackers	90
Hearty Wheat	4 crackers	180

	Serving Size	Sodium (mgs)
Sesame	4 crackers	105
Three Cracker Assortment	4 crackers	180
Toasted Wheat with Onion	4 crackers	110
Snack Sticks		
Cheddar Cheese	8 crackers	180
Original	8 crackers	180
Pumpernickel	8 crackers	180
Sesame	8 crackers	160
Thin Crackers		
Butter Flavored	4 crackers	100
Tiny Goldfish Crackers		
Cheddar Cheese	45 crackers	180
Original	45 crackers	180
Parmesan Cheese	45 crackers	250
Pizza Flavored	45 crackers	180
Pretzel	40 crackers	160
Frozen Products		
Croissant Pastry Pizza		
Cheese	1 pizza	730
Deluxe	1 pizza	940
Hamburger	1 pizza	1040
Pepperoni	1 pizza	810
Sausage	1 pizza	910
Fruit Squares		
Apple	1 square	170
Blueberry	1 square	190
Cherry	1 square	180
Layer Cakes		
Butterscotch Pecan	$1^5/_8$ oz	110
Chocolate Fudge	$1^5/_8$ oz	140
Chocolate Mint	$1^5/_8$ oz	140
Coconut	$1^5/_8$ oz	120
Devil's Food	$1^5/_8$ oz	120
German Chocolate	$1^5/_8$ oz	170

	Serving Size	Sodium (mgs)
Golden	1⅝ oz	110
Vanilla	1⅝ oz	115
Old Fashioned Cakes		
Butter Pound	1 oz	140
Carrot with Cream Cheese Icing	1⅛ oz	140
Old Fashioned Muffins		
Blueberry	1 muffin	250
Bran with Raisins	1 muffin	250
Carrot Walnut	1 muffin	220
Chocolate Chip	1 muffin	180
Cinnamon Swirl	1 muffin	170
Corn	1 muffin	260
Puff Pastry		
Apple Dumplings	3 oz	230
Apple Criss Cross Pastry	2 oz	140
Apple Turnovers	1 turnover	210
Apple Strudel	3 oz	210
Blueberry Turnovers	1 turnover	230
Cherry Turnovers	1 turnover	280
Patty Shells	1 shell	180
Peach Turnovers	1 turnover	250
Puff Pastry Sheets	¼ sheet	290
Raspberry Turnovers	1 turnover	260
Supreme Cakes		
Boston Cream	2⅞ oz	190
Chocolate	2⅞ oz	140
Dutch Chocolate	1¾ oz	115
Grand Marnier	1½ oz	85
Lemon Coconut	3 oz	220
Peach Melba	3⅛ oz	135
Pineapple Cream	2 oz	130
Raspberry Mocha	3⅛ oz	170
Strawberry Cream	2 oz	120

	Serving Size	Sodium (mgs)
Vegetables in Pastry		
Broccoli with Cheese	1 pastry	450
Cauliflower and Cheese Sauce	1 pastry	460
Rolls		
Butter Crescent	1 roll	150
Club, Brown 'n Serve	1 roll	200
French Style	1 roll	230
Golden Twist	1 roll	150
Hamburger	1 roll	240
Onion Sandwich Bun with Poppy Seeds	1 roll	260
Parker House	1 roll	80
Sandwich with Sesame Seeds	1 roll	220
Sourdough Style French	1 roll	230
Stuffing		
Corn Bread	1 oz	320
Cube	1 oz	430
Herb Seasoned	1 oz	410
PETER PAN. (*See entries under Peanut Butter*)		
PICKLES (*Vlasic—Campbell's*)		
Hot & Spicy Garden Mix	1 oz	380
Kosher Baby Dills	1 oz	210
Kosher Country Dills	1 oz	210
Kosher Dill Gherkins	1 oz	210
Kosher Dill Spears	1 oz	175
Lightly Spiced Cocktail Onions	1 oz	365
No Garlic Dills	1 oz	210
Original Dills	1 oz	375
Zesty Crunchy Dills	1 oz	250
Zesty Dill Spears	1 oz	230
Bread & Butter Pickles		
Bread & Butter Sweet Butter Chips	1 oz	160

	Serving Size	Sodium (mgs)
Bread & Butter Sweet Butter Stix	1 oz	110
Old Fashioned Bread & Butter Chunks	1 oz	120
Half-the-Salt Pickles		
Hamburger Dill Chips	1 oz	175
Kosher Crunchy Dills	1 oz	125
Kosher Dill Spears	1 oz	120
Sweet Butter Chips	1 oz	80
Pickled Peppers		
Hot Banana Pepper Rings	1 oz	465
Mexican Jalapeño Peppers	1 oz	380
Mild Cherry Peppers	1 oz	410
Mild Greek Pepperoncini	1 oz	450
Refrigerated Pickles		
Deli Bread & Butter Chunks	1 oz	120
Kosher Deli Dills	1 oz	290
PIES (*Banquet*)		
Cream Pies		
Banana	2.33 oz	146
Chocolate	2.33 oz	106
Coconut	2.33 oz	113
Lemon	2.33 oz	111
Strawberry	2.33 oz	112
Family Size Fruit Pies		
Apple	3.33 oz	282
Blackberry	3.33 oz	342
Blueberry	3.33 oz	342
Cherry	3.33 oz	258
Mincemeat	3.33 oz	361
Peach	3.33 oz	275
Pumpkin	3.33 oz	341
Pet Ritz (26 oz)		
Apple Pie	4.33 oz	385
Blueberry Pie	4.33 oz	330

	Serving Size	Sodium (mgs)
Cherry Pie	4.33 oz	330
Peach Pie	4.33 oz	320
PIE CRUSTS		
All Ready Pie Crust (Pillsbury)	⅛ 2-crust pie	310
Graham Cracker Pie Shells (Pet Ritz)	.83 oz	80
PILLSBURY. (*See specific entries, e.g.* *Vegetables, Frozen.*)		
PIZZA, FROZEN		
Celeste (*Quaker Oats Co.*)		
Canadian Style Bacon Pizza (9 oz)	1 pizza	1750
Canadian Style Bacon Pizza (19 oz)	¼ pizza	1030
Cheese Pizza (8½ oz)	1 pizza	920
Cheese Pizza (17¾ oz)	¼ pizza	740
Deluxe Pizza (8½ oz)	1 pizza	1500
Deluxe Pizza (22¼ oz)	¼ pizza	1050
Pepperoni Pizza (6¾ oz)	1 pizza	1560
Pepperoni Pizza (19 oz)	¼ pizza	1170
Sausage Pizza (7½ oz)	1 pizza	1510
Sausage Pizza (20 oz)	¼ pizza	1080
Sausage & Mushroom Pizza (8½ oz)	1 pizza	1490
Sausage & Mushroom Pizza (22½ oz)	¼ pizza	1140
Suprema Pizza (9 oz)	1 pizza	1860
Suprema Pizza (23 oz)	¼ pizza	1140
Pillsbury Frozen		
Fox Deluxe Pizza		
Cheese	⅓ pizza	520
Hamburger	⅓ pizza	470
Pepperoni	⅓ pizza	520
Sausage	⅓ pizza	530
Sausage & Pepperoni Combination	⅓ pizza	530
Heat 'n Eat Microwave Pizza		
Cheese	4.1 oz	670
Combination	4.9 oz	1190
Pepperoni	4.6 oz	1070

	Serving Size	Sodium (mgs)
Sausage	4.8 oz	1130
John's Pizza (8″)		
Cheese	1 pizza	1740
Deluxe with Sausage	1 pizza	1440
Sausage	1 pizza	1500
John's "3" Pack Pizza		
Cheese	1 pizza	1040
Sausage	1 pizza	910
Jeno's Crisp 'n Tasty Pizza		
Canadian Style Bacon	⅓ pizza	660
Cheese	⅓ pizza	650
Combination	⅓ pizza	750
Hamburger	⅓ pizza	670
Jeno's Extra Toppings Pizza		
Combination	¼ pizza	1000
Pepperoni	¼ pizza	1090
Sausage	¼ pizza	1000
Jeno's "4" Snack Size Pizza		
Cheese	1 pizza	620
Deluxe Sausage	1 pizza	560
Pepperoni	1 pizza	650
Sausage	1 pizza	560
Jeno's Microwave Sausage/Cheese Pizza Rolls	6 rolls (3 oz)	440
Jeno's Pizza Rolls		
Cheese	6 rolls (3 oz)	350
Combination Sausage & Pepperoni	6 rolls (3 oz)	380
Hamburger	6 rolls (3 oz)	280
Microwave Pepperoni/Cheese	6 rolls (3 oz)	440
Pepperoni & Cheese	6 rolls (3 oz)	390
Microwave French Bread Pizza		
Cheese	1 pc	570
Pepperoni	1 pc	1160
Sausage	1 pc	1000

	Serving Size	Sodium (mgs)
Sausage & Pepperoni Combination	1 pc	1140
Mr. P's Pizza		
Combination	1 pizza	1510
Golden Topping	1 pizza	1500
Hamburger	1 pizza	1510
Pepperoni	1 pizza	1730
Sausage	1 pizza	1470
Pillsbury Microwave Pizza		
Cheese	7.1 oz	1190
Combination	9 oz	1550
Pepperoni	8.5 oz	1550
Sausage	8.75 oz	1420
Snack Tray Pizza		
Cheese	4 snacks	440
Pepperoni	4 snacks	470
Sausage	4 snacks	430
Totino's Extra! Pizza		
Cheese	1/4 pizza	450
Pepperoni	1/4 pizza	700
Sausage	1/4 pizza	770
Sausage & Pepperoni Combination	1/4 pizza	800
Totino's Microwave Pizza		
Cheese	3.9 oz	630
Pepperoni	4 oz	1270
Sausage	4.2 oz	920
Sausage & Pepperoni Combination	4.2 oz	1090
Totino's Microwave Pizza (Large)		
Cheese	1/3 pizza	770
Hamburger	1/3 pizza	940
Pepperoni	1/3 pizza	1000
Sausage	1/3 pizza	860
Sausage & Pepperoni Combination	1/3 pizza	940
Totino's My Classic Pizza		
Canadian Style Bacon	1/4 pizza	830

	Serving Size	Sodium (mgs)
Deluxe Cheese	¼ pizza	810
Deluxe Combination	¼ pizza	1040
Deluxe Pepperoni	¼ pizza	1090
Deluxe Sausage	¼ pizza	980
Totino's Pan Pizza		
Pepperoni	¼ pizza	1230
Sausage	¼ pizza	1010
Sausage & Pepperoni Combination	¼ pizza	1180
Three Cheese	¼ pizza	850
Totino's Party Pizza		
Bacon	⅓ pizza	710
Canadian Style Bacon	⅓ pizza	670
Cheese	⅓ pizza	650
Hamburger	⅓ pizza	650
Mexican Style	⅓ pizza	600
Nacho	⅓ pizza	480
Pepperoni	⅓ pizza	720
Sausage	⅓ pizza	780
Sausage & Pepperoni Combination	⅓ pizza	770
Vegetable	⅓ pizza	630
Totino's Pizza Slices		
Cheese	1 piece	350
Combination	1 piece	630
Pepperoni	1 piece	530
Sausage	1 piece	540
Totino's Temptin' Toppings Pizza		
Bacon	⅓ pizza	850
Canadian Style Bacon	⅓ pizza	860
Cheese	⅓ pizza	840
Hamburger	⅓ pizza	880
Mexican Style	⅓ pizza	710
Pepperoni	⅓ pizza	930
Sausage	⅓ pizza	790
Sausage & Pepperoni Combination	⅓ pizza	890

	Serving Size	Sodium (mgs)
Vegetable	⅓ pizza	750

PLANTERS. (*See entries under Nuts.*)

POPCORN

	Serving Size	Sodium (mgs)
Orville Redenbacher's Gourmet Buttery Flavor	1 tbs	0
Orville Redenbacher's Gourmet Microwave Popcorn		
Butter Flavor	4 c popped	200
Caramel	2½ c popped	90
Cheddar Cheese	3 c popped	280
Nacho Cheese	3 c popped	400
Natural Flavor	4 c popped	260
Sour Cream & Onion	3 c popped	260
Orville Redenbacher's Gourmet Original Popping Corn		
Oil & Salt	4 c	700
Plain	4 c	0
Pillsbury		
Frozen Microwave		
Butter Flavored	3 c popped	270
Original Flavor	3 c popped	270
Salt Free	3 c popped	5
Pop Secret (General Mills)		
Butter Flavor	3 c popped	250
Natural Flavor	3 c popped	260
No Salt	3 c popped	0

POSTUM

	Serving Size	Sodium (mgs)
Coffee Flavor Instant Hot Beverage	6 fl oz	0
Instant Hot Beverage	6 fl oz	0

POTATO SIDE DISHES (*Pillsbury*)

	Serving Size	Sodium (mgs)
Stuffed Potato with Cheese Flavor Topping	5 oz	520
Stuffed Potato with Sour Cream & Chives	5 oz	580

	Serving Size	Sodium (mgs)
PROGRESSO. (*See entries under Beans, Canned.*)		
PUDDING AND PIE FILLING (*Jell-O*)		
Banana (8″ pie)	⅙ pie	120
Butterscotch	½ c	130
Chocolate	½ c	110
Chocolate Fudge	½ c	110
Coconut Cream	½ c	100
French Vanilla	½ c	125
Lemon (9″ pie)	⅙ pie	70
Milk Chocolate	½ c	110
Vanilla	½ c	110
Jell-O Sugar Free Pudding and Pie Filling		
Chocolate	½ c	110
Vanilla	½ c	140
Chocolate Mousse Pie	⅛ pie	190
Coconut Cream Pie	⅛ pie	210
PUDDING AND PIE MIX		
Jell-O		
Instant Pudding & Pie Mix		
Banana Cream	½ c	380
Butter Pecan	½ c	380
Butterscotch	½ c	420
Chocolate	½ c	460
Chocolate Fudge	½ c	420
Coconut Cream	½ c	300
French Vanilla	½ c	380
Lemon	½ c	340
Milk Chocolate	½ c	450
Pineapple Cream	½ c	340
Pistachio	½ c	380
Vanilla	½ c	380

	Serving Size	Sodium (mgs)
Sugar Free Instant Pudding & Pie Mix		
Banana	½ c	370
Butterscotch	½ c	360
Chocolate	½ c	350
Chocolate Fudge	½ c	300
Pistachio	½ c	370
Vanilla	½ c	360
Royal Instant Puddings		
Banana Cream	½ c	390
Butterscotch	½ c	390
Chocolate	½ c	390
Chocolate Mint	½ c	390
Chocolate Chocolate Chip	½ c	390
Dark 'n Sweet	½ c	390
Lemon	½ c	350
Pistachio Nut	½ c	350
Sugar Free Puddings		
Butterscotch	½ c	470
Chocolate	½ c	480
Vanilla	½ c	470
Toasted Butter Almond	½ c	350
Toasted Coconut	½ c	350
Vanilla	½ c	390
Royal No-Bake Pie Mixes		
Chocolate Mint Pie Mix	⅛ pie	280
Chocolate Mousse Pie Mix	⅛ pie	260
Lemon Meringue Pie Mix	⅛ pie	250
Lite Cheese Cake Mix	⅛ pie	280
Real Cheese Cake Mix	⅛ pie	370
Royal Puddings and Pie Fillings		
Banana Cream	½ c	210
Butterscotch	½ c	210

	Serving Size	Sodium (mgs)
Chocolate	½ c	150
Custard	½ c	115
Dark 'n Sweet	½ c	150
Flan with Caramel Sauce	½ c	115
Key Lime Pie Filling	½ c	120
Lemon Pie Filling	½ c	120
Vanilla	½ c	210
Vanilla Tapioca	½ c	150

R

	Serving Size	Sodium (mgs)
RELISH (*Vlasic*)		
Dill Relish	1 oz	415
Hamburger Relish	1 oz	255
Hot Dog Relish	1 oz	255
Sweet Relish	1 oz	220
RICE DISHES		
Minute Rice (prepared without salt or butter)	⅔ c	0
Minute Rice Mix		
Drumstick (prepared with salted butter)	½ c	650
Fried Rice (prepared with oil)	½ c	690
Long Grain & Wild (prepared with salted butter)	½ c	570
Rib Roast (prepared with salted butter)	½ c	720
Pillsbury Rice Originals		
Italian Blend White Rice & Spinach in Cheese Sauce	½ c	400
Long Grain White and Wild Rice	½ c	550
Rice Jubilee	½ c	340
Rice 'n Broccoli in Flavored Cheese Sauce	½ c	510
Rice Pilaf	½ c	520

	Serving Size	Sodium (mgs)
Rice with Herb Butter Sauce	½ c	390
ROSALITA PRODUCTS (*Beatrice/Hunt-Wesson*)		
Rosalita Enchilada Sauce	3 oz	430
Rosalita Refried Beans	4 oz	460
Rosalita Refried Beans with Green Chilies	4 oz	430
Rosalita Spicy Refried Beans	4 oz	440
Rosalita Taco Shells	1 shell	0
Rosalita Vegetarian Refried Beans	4 oz	460
ROYAL. (*See entries under Gelatin.*)		

S

	Serving Size	Sodium (mgs)
SALAD DRESSINGS		
Good Seasons Salad Dressing Mix		
Bleu Cheese and Herbs*	1 tbs	160
Buttermilk, Farm Style†	1 tbs	95
Cheese Garlic	1 tbs	170
Cheese Italian	1 tbs	135
Classic Herb	1 tbs	150
Garlic & Herbs	1 tbs	190
Italian	1 tbs	150
Lemon and Herbs	1 tbs	140
Lite Italian	1 tbs	180
Lite Zesty Italian	1 tbs	130
Mild Italian	1 tbs	190
No Oil Italian Dressing Mix‡	1 tbs	30
Zesty Italian	1 tbs	120
SALADS, FRESH CHEF (*Campbell's*)		
Chicken with Almonds	4½ oz	580
Ham & Cheddar Cheese	4½ oz	850
Holiday Coleslaw	44 oz	240

*Unless otherwise stated, made with vinegar, salad oil, and water
†Prepared with whole milk and mayonnaise
‡Prepared with vinegar and water, no oil added

	Serving Size	Sodium (mgs)
SAUCES*		
Hellmann's		
Tartar Sauce	1 tbs	220
Sandwich Spread	1 tbs	170
Nabisco		
A.1. Steak	1 tbs	280
Escoffier Sauce Diable	1 tbs	160
Escoffier Sauce Robert	1 tbs	70
Steak Supreme Steak Sauce	1 tbs	25
Ocean Spray		
CranOrange Sauce	100 gm	10
CranRaspberry Sauce	100 gm	15
Jellied Cranberry Sauce	100 gm	15
Whole Berry Sauce	100 gm	15
Van de Kamp's Tartar Sauce (+ ⅓ c mayonnaise)	1 oz	0
SAUERKRAUT (*Vlasic Old Fashioned*)	1 oz	280
SEAFOOD, FROZEN		
Mrs. Paul's		
Catfish Strips	4 oz	290
Combination Seafood Platter	9 oz	1220
Crispy Crunchy Breaded Fish Fillets	2 fillets	550
Crispy Crunchy Fish Sticks	2 fillets	350
Crispy Crunchy Flounder Fillets	2 fillets	500
Crispy Crunchy Haddock Fillets	2 fillets	410
Crispy Crunchy Ocean Perch Fillets	2 fillets	460
40 Crunchy Fish Sticks	4 sticks	340
Deviled Crabs	1 cake	390
Deviled Crab Miniatures	3½ oz	480
Fish Cakes	2 cakes	840
Fish Cake Thins	2 cakes	1210
Fried Scallops	3½ oz	480

*See also Hunt's Products.

	Serving Size	Sodium (mgs)
Fried Shrimp	3 oz	430
Light Fillets, Catfish	1 fillet	389
Light Fillets, Cod	1 fillet	412
Light Fillets, Flounder	1 fillet	536
Light Fillets, Haddock	1 fillet	456
Light Fillets, Perch	1 fillet	391
Light Fillets, Pollock	1 fillet	530
Light Fillets, Sole	1 fillet	536
Stuffed Fillets, Broccoli	1 fillet	581
Stuffed Fillets, Cheese	1 fillet	520
Light Seafood Entrées		
Fish au Gratin	9 oz	1100
Fish and Pasta	9 oz	870
Fish Dijon	8¾ oz	430
Fish Florentine	8 oz	580
Fish Mornay	9 oz	660
Shrimp Cajun Style	9 oz	860
Shrimp and Clams with Linguini	10 oz	790
Shrimp Primavera	9½ oz	980
Tuna Pasta Casserole	10 oz	960
Prepared/Battered		
Batter Dipped Fish Fillets	2 fillets	581
Crunchy Batter Fish Fillets	2 fillets	810
Crunchy Batter Fish Sticks	4 sticks	590
Crunchy Batter Flounder Fillets	2 fillets	790
Crunchy Batter Haddock Fillets	2 fillets	670
Fried Clams	2½ oz	380
Supreme Light Batter Fish Fillets	1 fillet	540
Additional Prepared Seafood Products		
Au Naturel Cod Fillets	5 oz	200
Au Naturel Flounder Fillets	5 oz	210
Au Naturel Haddock Fillets	5 oz	230
Au Naturel Perch Fillets	5 oz	200
Au Naturel Sole Fillets	5 oz	170

	Serving Size	Sodium (mgs)
Buttered Fish Fillets	2 fillets	390
Van de Kamp's Frozen Foods		
Batter-Dipped		
Fish & Chips	1 pkg (10 oz)	610
Fish Fillets	1 pc	230
Fish Kabobs	4 oz	430
Fish Sticks	4 pcs	330
Haddock	2 pcs	430
Halibut	3 pcs	440
Ocean Perch	2 pcs	510
Breaded		
Clams	2½ oz	320
Country Seasoned	1 pc	335
Fish Nuggets	4 oz	320
Fish Sticks	4 pcs	300
Haddock Fillets	1 pc	160
Ocean Perch Fillets	1 pc	115
MW Lightly Breaded		
Cod	5 oz	370
Flounder	5 oz	410
Haddock	5 oz	310
Halibut	4 oz	520
Ocean Perch	5 oz	330
Sole	5 oz	410
Today's Catch		
Baby Sole	5 oz	150
Cod	5 oz	220
Fish Fillets	5 oz	110
Flounder	5 oz	170
Haddock	5 oz	180
Perch	5 oz	150
SEGO LITE LIQUID DIET PRODUCTS		
Sego Lite Chocolate	1 can (10 fl oz)	490

	Serving Size	Sodium (mgs)
Sego Lite Chocolate Jamocha Almond	1 can (10 fl oz)	475
Sego Lite Chocolate Malt	1 can (10 fl oz)	475
Sego Lite Double Chocolate	1 can (10 fl oz)	475
Sego Lite Dutch Chocolate	1 can (10 fl oz)	475
Sego Lite French Vanilla	1 can (10 fl oz)	390
Sego Lite Strawberry	1 can (10 fl oz)	390
Sego Lite Vanilla	1 can (10 fl oz)	490

SHAKE 'N BAKE SEASONING MIXTURE

	Serving Size	Sodium (mgs)
Country Mild Recipe	½ pouch	500
Italian Herb Recipe	¼ pouch	640
Original Barbecue Recipe for Chicken	¼ pouch	840
Original Barbecue Recipe for Pork	¼ pouch	700
Original Recipe for Chicken	¼ pouch	450
Original Recipe for Fish	¼ pouch	410
Original Recipe for Pork	¼ pouch	600

SNACK FOOD
General Mills

	Serving Size	Sodium (mgs)
Bugles	1 oz	290
Nacho Cheese Bugles	1 oz	270

Nabisco Snacks
Doo Dads

	Serving Size	Sodium (mgs)
Cheddar 'n Herb	½ c	400
Original	½ c	360
Zesty Cheese	½ c	420

Mister Salty

	Serving Size	Sodium (mgs)
Butter Flavor Rings Pretzels	23 pcs	570

	Serving Size	Sodium (mgs)
Butter Flavor Sticks Pretzels	90 pcs	620
Dutch Pretzels	2 pcs	440
Junior Pretzels	29 pcs	500
Pretzel Sticks	90 pcs	620
Pretzel Mini	16 pcs	450
Pretzel Mini Mix	23 pcs	480
Pretzel Rings	22 pcs	510
Pretzel Twists	5 pcs	590
Veri-Thin Pretzel Sticks	45 pcs	770
Planter Snacks		
Cheez Balls	1 oz	270
Cheez Curls	1 oz	290
Corn Chips	1 oz	160
Microwave Popcorn (butter)	3 c popped	560
Microwave Popcorn (natural)	3 c popped	560
Peanut Bar	1.6 oz	70
Popcorn	3 c popped	0
Potato Crunchies	1¼ oz	310
Pretzels	1 oz	700
Round Toast Crackers	4 sandwiches	270
Sour Cream & Onion Puffs	1 oz	300
Square Cheese Crackers	4 sandwiches	270
Sweet 'n Crunchy Peanut Candy	1 oz	70

SOUPS, CANNED
Campbell's Condensed

Asparagus, Cream of	All Camp-	840
Bean with Bacon	bell's Soup	860
Beef	products	840
Beef Broth (bouillon)	serving size	820
Beef Noodle	are based	880
Black Bean	on 100 gm	950
Beefy Mushroom	as packaged.	960
Celery, Cream of		860
Cheddar Cheese		750

	Serving Size	Sodium (mgs)
Chicken Alphabet	All Camp-	850
Chicken Broth	bell's Soup	750
Chicken Broth and Noodles	products	850
Chicken Broth and Rice	serving size	850
Chicken, Cream of	are based on	850
Chicken 'n Dumplings	100 gm as	980
Chicken Gumbo	packaged.	900
Chicken Noodle		910
Chicken NoodleO's		840
Chicken Noodle, Homestyle		920
Chicken with Rice		820
Chicken & Stars		820
Chicken Vegetable		880
Chili Beef		980
Clam Chowder, Manhattan-Style		840
Clam Chowder, New England Style		880
Clam Chowder, New England Style (made with milk)		930
Consommé (Beef), Gelatin Added		770
Creamy Chicken Mushroom		940
Curly Noodle with Chicken		960
French Onion		920
Golden Mushroom		880
Green Pea		830
Meatball Alphabet		950
Minestrone		910
Mushroom, Cream of		820
Nacho Cheese		680
Noodles and Ground Beef		820
Onion, Cream of		830
Onion, Cream of (made with water and milk)		860
Oyster Stew		850
Oyster Stew (made with milk)		900

	Serving Size	Sodium (mgs)
Pepper Pot	All Camp-	960
Potato, Cream of	bell's Soup	880
Potato, Cream of (made with water and milk)	products serving size	910
Scotch Broth	are based on	870
Shrimp, Cream of	100 gm as	790
Shrimp, Cream of (made with milk)	packaged	850
Spanish Style Vegetable (Gazpacho)		590
Split Pea with Ham & Bacon		790
Tomato		660
Tomato (made with milk)		710
Tomato Bisque		820
Tomato, Homestyle, Cream of (made with milk)		830
Tomato Rice, Old-Fashioned		760
Turkey Noodle		870
Vegetable		800
Vegetable Beef		820
Vegetable, Homestyle		890
Vegetable, Vegetarian		800
Wonton		880
Zesty Tomato		790

Canned Semi-Condensed Soups for One

	Serving Size	Sodium (mgs)
Old Fashioned Bean with Ham	7¾ oz	1340
Burly Vegetable Beef & Bacon	7¾ oz	1440
Clam Chowder, New England	7¾ oz	1360
Clam Chowder, New England (made with milk)	7¾ oz	1410
Full Flavored Chicken Vegetable		1500
Golden Chicken and Noodles	7¾ oz	1450
Old World Vegetable	7¾ oz	1470
Savory Cream of Mushroom	7½ oz	1500
Tomato Royale	7¾ oz	1080

	Serving Size	Sodium (mgs)
Chunky Soups Individual Serving Size		
(*Ready to Serve*)		
Chunky Beef with Country Vegetables	10¾ oz	1080
Chunky Stroganoff Style Beef	10¾ oz	1290
Chunky Chicken Noodle with Mushrooms	10¾ oz	1140
Chunky Chili Beef with Beans	10¾ oz	1150
Chunky Clam Chowder (Manhattan-Style)	10¾ oz	1280
Chunky New England Clam Chowder	10¾ oz	1180
Chunky Creamy Mushroom	10¾ oz	1280
Chunky Fisherman Chowder	10¾ oz	1320
Chunky Ham 'n Butter Bean	10¾ oz	1180
Chunky Old Fashioned Bean with Ham	11 oz	1110
Chunky Old Fashioned Vegetable Beef	10¾ oz	1130
Chunky Old Fashioned Chicken	10¾ oz	1190
Chunky Sirloin Burger	10¾ oz	1270
Chunky Split Pea 'n Ham	10¾ oz	1070
Chunky Steak and Potato	10¾ oz	1110
Chunky Vegetable	10¾ oz	1100
Chunky Soup (*19 oz ready to serve*)		
Chunky Beef	9½ oz	950
Chunky Chicken Noodle	9½ oz	1010
Chunky Chicken Rice	9½ oz	1050
Chunky Chicken Vegetable	9½ oz	1100
Chunky Chili Beef	9¾ oz	1000
Chunky Clam Chowder (Manhattan-Style)	9½ oz	1080
Chunky New England Clam Chowder	9½ oz	1040
Chunky Creamy Chicken Mushroom	9⅜ oz	1260
Chunky Creamy Mushroom	9⅜ oz	1140

	Serving Size	Sodium (mgs)
Chunky Fisherman Chowder	9½ oz	1160
Chunky Mediterranean Vegetable	9½ oz	1020
Chunky Minestrone	9½ oz	860
Chunky Old Fashioned Bean with Ham	9⅝ oz	960
Chunky Old Fashioned Chicken	9½ oz	1040
Chunky Old Fashioned Vegetable Beef	9½ oz	1000
Chunky Sirloin Burger	9½ oz	1100
Chunky Split Pea with Ham	9½ oz	940
Chunky Steak 'n Potato	9½ oz	370
Chunky Turkey Vegetable	9⅜ oz	1060
Chunky Vegetable	9½ oz	970
Creamy Natural Soups Condensed (*Campbell's*)		
Asparagus (made with milk)	as	710
Broccoli (made with milk)	packaged	570
Cauliflower (made with milk)		850
Potato (made with milk)		510
Spinach (made with milk)		700
Home Cookin' Soups (*Ready to Serve*)		
Chicken with Broad Egg Noodles	10¾ oz	1020
Country Vegetable	10¾ oz	1130
Hearty Lentil	10¾ oz	940
Old World Minestrone	10¾ oz	1200
Split Pea with Ham	10¾ oz	1180
Vegetable Beef	10¾ oz	1110
Low Sodium Soups (*Ready to Serve*)		
Chicken Broth	19½ oz	70
Chicken with Noodles	10¾ oz	85
Chicken Beef & Mushroom (chunky)	10¾ oz	65
Chunky Chicken Vegetable	10¾ oz	95
Chunky Vegetable Beef	10¾ oz	60
Cream of Mushroom	10½ oz	55

	Serving Size	Sodium (mgs)
French Onion	10½ oz	50
Tomato with Tomato Pieces	10½ oz	40
Split Pea	10¾ oz	25
Quality Soup Mix (*Dry*)		
Cheddar Cheese	1 pack	820
Chicken Noodle with White Chicken Meat	1 pack	780
Chicken Rice	1 pack	810
Noodle	1 pack	730
Onion	½ pack	730
Onion Mushroom	½ pack	700
College Inn Broths (*Nabisco*)		
Beef	1 c	1280
Chicken	1 c	1320
Manischewitz Soups		
Vegetable Soup Mix	6 oz	85
Borscht with Beets	8 oz	660
Low Calorie Borscht	8 oz	725
Minestrone Soup Mix	6 oz	160
Split Pea Soup Mix	6 oz	320
SPAGHETTI SAUCE (*Prego*)		
Al Fresco Garden Tomato Sauce	4 oz	630
Al Fresco Garden Tomato Sauce with Mushrooms	4 oz	560
Al Fresco Garden Tomato Sauce with Peppers	4 oz	560
Prego Plus with Beef Sirloin w/Onion	4 oz	420
Prego Plus with Mushrooms and Chuck	4 oz	400
Prego Plus with Sausage & Green Peppers	4 oz	480
Prego Plus with Veal & Sliced Mushrooms	4 oz	380
Spaghetti Sauce	4 oz	670

	Serving Size	Sodium (mgs)
Spaghetti Sauce Meat Flavored	4 oz	920
Spaghetti Sauce with Mushrooms	4 oz	640
Spaghetti Sauce No-Salt-Added	4 oz	25
STARCH		
Argo and Kingsfords Corn Starch	1 tbs	0
STRUDEL (*Pillsbury*)		
Apple Spice	1	190
Blueberry	1	200
Breakfast Pastries	1	200
Cherry	1	200
Cinnamon	1	200
Raspberry	1	200
Strawberry	1	200
STUFFING		
Stove Top Stuffing Mix		
Americana New England	½ c	560
Americana San Francisco	½ c	560
Beef	½ c	500
Chicken Flavor	½ c	480
Cornbread	½ c	490
Long Grain Wild Rice	½ c	470
Pork	½ c	540
Savory Herbs	½ c	500
Turkey	½ c	550
With Rice	½ c	480
Stove Top Flexible Serving Stuffing Mix		
Chicken Flavor	½ c	510
Cornbread Flavor	½ c	530
Homestyle Herb	½ c	470
Stuffing Originals (*Pillsbury*)		
Chicken	½ c	570
Mushroom	½ c	780
Cornbread	½ c	660

	Serving Size	Sodium (mgs)
Wild Rice	½ c	540
SWANSON. (*See entries under Dinners, Frozen.*)		
SYRUP		
Golden Griddle (Best Foods)	1 tbs	15
Karo Dark Corn Syrup	1 tbs	40
Karo Light Corn Syrup	1 tbs	30
Karo Pancake Syrup	1 tbs	35
Vermont Maid Syrup	1 tbs	5

T

	Serving Size	Sodium (mgs)
TACO SHELLS (*Pillsbury*)		
Corn	1 shell	65
Flour	1 shell	70
TANG. (*See entries under Drink Mixes.*)		
TOASTER MUFFINS		
(*Pillsbury*)		
Apple Spice	1	120
Banana Nut	1	80
Old Fashioned Corn	1	250
Raisin Bran	1	220
Wild Maine Blueberry	1	120
TOASTER PASTRIES		
(*Nabisco*)		
Apple	1 pc	170
Blueberry	1 pc	200
Cherry	1 pc	200
Frosted Blueberry	1 pc	200
Frosted Brown Sugar Cinnamon	1 pc	170
Frosted Cherry	1 pc	200
Frosted Fudge	1 pc	220
Frosted Strawberry	1 pc	200
Strawberry	1 pc	200

	Serving Size	Sodium (mgs)
TOMATO PASTE. (*See entries under Hunt's Products.*)		
TORTILLAS (*Pillsbury*)		
Corn	1 tortilla	5
Flour (7 inch)	1 tortilla	110
TROPICANA. (*See entries under Juice, Canned.*)		

V

	Serving Size	Sodium (mgs)
VAN CAMP'S. (*See entries under Beans, Canned.*)		
VEGETABLES, CANNED (*Pillsbury*)		
Asparagus Cuts (8 and 10½ oz)	½ c	450
Asparagus Spears	½ c	340
Blackeye Peas	½ c	350
Butter Beans	½ c	420
Chili Beans	½ c	660
Cream Style Corn (8.5 and 17 oz)	½ c	320 or 360
Cut Sweet Potatoes	½ c	45
Cut Wax Beans	½ c	330
Early June Peas (8.5 and 17 oz)	½ c	380
Four Bean Salad	½ c	850
French Style Cut Green Beans (8 and 16 oz)	½ c	310
Garbanzo Beans	½ c	420
Garden Salad	½ c	600
German Style Green Bean Salad	½ c	730
German Style Potato Salad	½ c	830
Golden Shoe Peg Corn (17 oz)	½ c	270
Golden Whole Kernel Corn	½ c	190
Great Northern Beans	½ c	420
Green Beans	½ c	380

	Serving Size	Sodium (mgs)
Green Beans, 1½" Cut (8¼ and 16 oz)	½ c	310
Home Style Potato Salad	½ c	750
Joan of Arc Canned Vegetables	½ c	420
Kitchen Cut Green Beans (8½ and 16 oz)	½ c	260
Le Sueur Asparagus Spears (15 and 19 oz)	½ c	390
Le Sueur Whole Kernel Corn (17 oz)	½ c	290
Macaroni Salad	½ c	850
Mashed Sweet Potatoes	½ c	60
Mexicorn with Peppers (7 and 12 oz)	½ c	330
Mini Sweet Peas (8½ and 17 oz)	½ c	420
Mushroom Pieces & Stems, Buttons (2 oz)	2 oz	260
Mushrooms, B IN B (3 and 6 oz)	2 oz	530
Mushrooms in Butter Sauce (3 oz)	2 oz	530
Navy Beans	½ c	550
Pinto Beans	½ c	660
Pork and Beans	½ c	660
Pumpkin	½ c	25
Red Kidney Beans, Dark	½ c	340
Red Kidney Beans, Light	½ c	390
Small Red Beans	½ c	450
Sweet Peas (8½ and 17 oz)	½ c	240 or 370
Sweet Peas & Onions (17 oz)	½ c	550
Sweet Potatoes in Orange Pineapple Sauce	½ c	60
Three Bean Salad (17 oz)	½ c	540 or 920
White Shoepeg Corn Vacuum Pack (7 and 12 oz)	½ c	270
Whole Kernel Corn Vacuum Pack (7 and 12 oz)	½ c	230

	Serving Size	Sodium (mgs)
Whole Sweet Potatoes Packed in Heavy Syrup	½ c	40
VEGETABLES, FROZEN		
Bird's Eye		
Combination Vegetables		
Baby Brussels Sprouts with Cheese Sauce	4.5 oz	420
Broccoli & Cauliflower with Creamy Italian Cheese Sauce	4.5 oz	390
Broccoli, Carrots, Pasta Twists	3.3 oz	270
Broccoli, Cauliflower, Carrot/ Cheese Sauce	5 oz	380
Broccoli/Cheese Sauce	5 oz	490
Broccoli/Creamy Italian Cheese Sauce	4.5 oz	390
Cauliflower with Cheese Sauce	5 oz	480
Corn, Green Beans, Pasta Curls	3.3 oz	280
Creamed Spinach	3 oz	310
French Green Beans/Toasted Almonds	3 oz	340
Green Peas and Pearl Onions	3.3 oz	440
Green Peas & Potatoes with Cream Sauce	2.6 oz	390
Green Peas with Cream Sauce	2.6 oz	370
Mixed Vegetables with Onion Sauce	2.6 oz	340
Peas & Pearl Onions/Cheese Sauce	5 oz	440
Rice & Green Peas with Mushroom Sauce	2.3 oz	320
Small Onions with Cream Sauce	3 oz	350
Deluxe Vegetables		
Artichoke Hearts	3 oz	40
Beans, Whole Green	3 oz	0

	Serving Size	Sodium (mgs)
Broccoli, Baby Spears	3.3 oz	15
Broccoli Florets	3.3 oz	20
Carrots, Baby Peas, & Pearl Onions	3.3 oz	60
Carrots, Whole Baby	3.3 oz	45
Corn, Tender Sweet	3.3 oz	0
Peas, Tiny Tender	3.3 oz	120
International Vegetables with Seasoned Sauces		
Bavarian Style Green Beans & Spaetzle	3.3 oz	420
Chinese Style	3.3 oz	370
Chow Mein Style	3.3 oz	370
Italian Style	3.3 oz	570
Japanese Style	3.3 oz	490
Mandarin Style	3.3 oz	390
New England Style	3.3 oz	410
Pasta Primavera Style	3.3 oz	340
San Francisco Style	3.3 oz	400
Regular Vegetables		
Asparagus Cuts	3.3 oz	5
Asparagus Spears	3.3 oz	0
Beans, Cut Green	3 oz	0
Beans, French Cut Green	3 oz	0
Beans, Italian Green	3 oz	0
Beans, Baby Lima	3.3 oz	115
Beans, Fordhook Lima	3.3 oz	100
Broccoli, Chopped	3.3 oz	15
Broccoli Cuts	3.3 oz	25
Broccoli Spears	3.3 oz	20
Brussels Sprouts	3.3 oz	15
Cauliflower	3.3 oz	20
Corn, Big Ears on the Cob	1 ear	0
Corn, Little Ears on the Cob	2 ears	0

	Serving Size	Sodium (mgs)
Corn on the Cob	3.3 oz	0
Corn, Sweet	3.3 oz	0
Green Peas	3.3 oz	130
Mixed Vegetables	3.3 oz	40
Onions, Small Whole	4 oz	10
Spinach, Chopped	3.3 oz	90
Spinach, Whole Leaf	3.3 oz	90
Squash, Cooked Winter	4 oz	0
Stir-Fry Vegetables		
Chinese Style	3.3 oz	540
Japanese Style	3.3 oz	510
International Rice Recipes		
French Style	3.3 oz	610
Italian Style	3.3 oz	350
Spanish Style	3.3 oz	540
Farm Fresh Mixtures		
Broccoli, Baby Carrots, & Water Chestnuts	3.2 oz	25
Broccoli, Cauliflower, and Carrots	3.2 oz	25
Broccoli, Corn, and Red Peppers	3.2 oz	15
Broccoli, Green Beans, Pearl Onions, & Red Peppers	3.2 oz	15
Broccoli, Red Peppers, Bamboo Shoots, & Straw Mushrooms	3.2 oz	15
Brussels Sprouts, Cauliflower, & Carrots	3.2 oz	20
Cauliflower, Baby Whole Carrots, Snow Pea Pods	3.2 oz	25
Mrs. Paul's		
Candied Sweet Potatoes	4 oz	60
Candied Sweets and Apples	4 oz	70
Corn Fritters	2 fritters	630
Crispy Onion Rings	2½ oz	270

	Serving Size	Sodium (mgs)
Eggplant Parmigiana	5 oz	600
Light Batter Zucchini Sticks	3 oz	440
Pillsbury		
Broccoli Cuts	½ c	10
Brussels Sprouts	½ c	10
Cauliflower Cuts	½ c	15
Early June Peas	½ c	170
Frozen Like Fresh Broccoli Mini-spears	½ c	10
Lima Beans	½ c	30
Mixed Vegetables	½ c	30
Niblets Corn	½ c	5
Niblets 4 ear corn-on-the-cob	1 ear	20
Niblets 6 ear corn-on-the-cob	½ c	20
Polybag Green Beans	½ c	10
Spinach	½ c	60
Sweet Peas	½ c	110
White Shoepeg Corn	½ c	0
Butter Sauce Vegetables		
Baby Lima Beans	½ c	460
Broccoli, Cauliflower, Carrots	½ c	340
Broccoli Spears	½ c	340
Brussels Sprouts	½ c	320
Cauliflower	½ c	310
Cut Green Beans	½ c	300
French Style Green Beans	½ c	360
Le Sueur Early Peas	½ c	590
Le Sueur Mini Peas, Pea Pods, & Water Chestnuts	½ c	410
Le Sueur Peas, Onions, & Carrots	½ c	470
Mixed Vegetables	½ c	370
Niblets Corn in Butter Sauce	½ c	280
Sweet Peas	½ c	490

	Serving Size	Sodium (mgs)
White Shoepeg Corn in Butter Sauce	½ c	340
Cream and Cheese Sauce Vegetables		
Baby Brussels Sprouts in Cheese Flavored Sauce	½ c	450
Broccoli Cauliflower Carrots in Cheese Flavored Sauce	½ c	490
Broccoli in Cheese	½ c	530
Broccoli in White Cheddar Flavored Sauce	½ c	450
Cauliflower in White Cheddar Flavored Sauce	½ c	420
Creamed Spinach	½ c	480
Cream Style Corn	½ c	370
Peas in Cream Sauce	½ c	320
Harvest Fresh Vegetables		
Broccoli Spears	½ c	200
Cut Broccoli	½ c	200
Cut Green Beans	½ c	150
Early June Peas	½ c	170
Lima Beans	½ c	150
Niblets Corn	½ c	150
Mixed Vegetables	½ c	170
Spinach	½ c	360
Sweet Peas	½ c	220
White Shoepeg Corn	½ c	270
Harvest Get Togethers Vegetables		
Broccoli Cauliflower Medley	½ c	470
Broccoli Fanfare	½ c	470
Cauliflower Carrot Bonanza	½ c	290

	Serving Size	Sodium (mgs)
Valley Combinations Polybag Vegetables		
Broccoli Carrot Fanfare	½ c	30
Broccoli Cauliflower Supreme	½ c	30
Cauliflower Green Bean Festival	½ c	30
Corn Broccoli Bounty	½ c	15
Sweet Pea Cauliflower Medley	½ c	60
Valley Combination Dual Pouch Vegetables		
American Style Vegetables	½ c	340
Broccoli Cauliflower Medley	½ c	430
Broccoli Fanfare	½ c	430
Italian Style Vegetables	½ c	310
Japanese Style Vegetables	½ c	340
Le Sueur Style Vegetables	½ c	340
Mexican Style Vegetables	½ c	540
VINEGARS		
Red Wine	1 oz	20
Red Wine/Garlic	1 oz	20
White Wine	1 oz	10

W

	Serving Size	Sodium (mgs)
WATER, BOTTLED		
Domestic		
Calistoga	1 liter	150.0
Crystal Geyser	1 liter	160.0
Mendocino	1 liter	200.0
Mountain Valley	1 liter	2.9
Poland Spring	1 liter	3.0
Imported		
Apollinaris	1 liter	630.5
Badoit	1 liter	13.8
Evian	1 liter	.5
Fuiggi	1 liter	6.0
Perrier	1 liter	14.0
Ramlosa (Sweden)	1 liter	240.0
San Pellegrino	1 liter	46.5
Spa (Belgium)	1 liter	2.5
Vichy	1 liter	1200.0
Vittel Grande Source	1 liter	3.8

Y

	Serving Size	Sodium (mgs)
YOGURT (*Yoplait*)		
Original		
Fruit Flavor	6 oz	105
Plain	6 oz	120
Custard Style		
Fruit Flavors	6 oz	95
Mixed Berry	6 oz	95
Vanilla	6 oz	119
Lowfat Breakfast Yogurt From Yo-plait		
Apple Cinnamon	6 oz	90
Berries	6 oz	95
Cherry with Almonds	6 oz	90
Strawberry Banana	6 oz	90
Tropical Fruits	6 oz	90
Yoplait 150 Fruit Flavors	6 oz	95
Yoplait Yo Creme		
Amaretto Almond	5 oz	80
Bavarian Chocolate	5 oz	95
Cherries Jubilee	5 oz	80
Raspberries and Creme	5 oz	80
Strawberries Romanoff	5 oz	80